Recipe...
Angelo
Vicki Ba...

Edited by
Marjorie and Clyde Childress

Designed by
Craig Bergquist

Photography by
Clyde Childress

W9-BXD-742

Adventures in Mexican Cooking

Contents

Culture and cooking

Mexico and the United States share more than a common border. In a very real way the two nations overlap. This gives us some familiarity with Mexican cooking. We hope this book will expand that familiarity, and deepen your appreciation for a great cuisine.

Half of all the food you eat probably had its origin in pre-Columbian America. Indeed, long before the Spanish expeditions to this New World, Mexico had developed a highly organized system of agriculture. It had also developed a companion system of sophisticated culinary art. And this art was based on foodstuffs that were simply unknown to either Europe or Asia.

It is hard to imagine what cooking in Europe was like before the introduction of beans, squash, potatoes, peppers, tomatoes and all the other New World contributions.

But of all the indigenous plants, corn (or *maíz)* was the most important contributor to the sustenance of the people. Corn had been cultivated and tended for so long that, according to myth, it was the very stuff from which the gods created the people.

The strength and ongoing force of the pre-Hispanic cooking system is clearly demonstrated by its dominant influence on the cuisine of contemporary Mexico.

There are many reasons why Mexican cooking has retained so much of its pre-Hispanic character; the most likely reason is, simply, that people through the ages have liked the taste. It can't be that the traditions were retained for cooking convenience, since the dishes are neither quick nor easy. Such fare can provide a fast and convenient way to eat, as witness the number of

◁

These familiar vegetables, staples in your garden, were staples in the gardens of Mexico when the originals of these ceramic pieces were made over 1000 years ago.

packaged snack foods sold in the United States that are adaptations of traditional Mexican fare.

Historically, we can assume that another reason native Mexican cooking methods were not smothered under the weight of European methods was that there were many Indians and they already knew how to cook. Indeed, in 1518, when Juan de Grijalva sailed up the eastern coasts of the land he would name New Spain, he reported that he found cities "so large that Seville [then the world's most splendid trading port] could not show to better advantage."

Another and probably more crucial reason for the continuity of indigenous cooking methods was the lay of the Mexican land itself. The mountains, which cover two-thirds of the land area, isolated various parts of Mexico, impeding the penetration of new food ingredients and cooking methods from Spain. This isolation provided the

necessary time for the newly arriving kitchen techniques and ingredients to meld slowly with the traditional Indian methods.

More than recipes

In this book, we would like most of all to give you a lot of Mexican recipes, both traditional and contemporary. Our hope is you will enjoy the dishes so much that they become a part of your regular repertoire. We would like to tell you considerably more about Mexican cooking than just "how to do it."

In Mexico, there is still a direct and vital link between the production and consumption of food — a link that has become obscured for most of us. In this book, we hope to help rekindle some of the reverence for food and for the natural world that sustains us all. It is a reverence that has been and still is deeply rooted in the native culture of Mexico.

Market day in Huachinango is Saturday: Ten city blocks of stretched awnings and the merchandise under them will be gone without a trace on Sunday morning.

These fields of Mexico are too steep to be worked by machines. Most of the work is done by manpower, with some help from burros and horses.

Although mechanized farming methods are used in many areas of Mexico, much of the land remains unsuited to such methods, and yokes of oxen still plow rocky fields that would demolish most modern machines.

The steep mountain slopes must also be farmed if the people are to eat. Such fields must be worked by men with the help of horses and burros, sturdy creatures that can take a firm foothold on a steep mountainside. Of course, the men may ride to their farm jobs on a bus, and the produce may be hauled to market on trucks.

In fact, buses and trucks may well be the most potent forces for change operating in Mexico today. The fish caught in Vera Cruz this morning will be in Mexico City (or even Guadalajara, 700 miles away) tomorrow.

The trucks, exhaust cutouts wide open, roaring like Gatling guns up the difficult grades of the Sierra Oriental with loads of sweet oranges, carry much more than oranges: they carry truck driver appetites for home cooking. Thus, the roadside eateries that cater to their needs must offer more than the standard dishes of their area.

As the country's population and produce become more mobile, cuisine changes. Already one finds dishes that were once regional specialties far from their homes. Sometimes they've traveled well, but sometimes it seems they've only brought their names.

For all the forces that are tending to homogenize the cooking of Mexico, there are also strong forces working to maintain the centuries-old traditions. There are still large areas in the country that are out of reach of the road system, and still larger areas touched only by difficult roads. The people in these areas necessarily live, eat and cook largely with the same ingredients and by the same methods that have been used since the time of the Aztec lords.

The milpa

The word *milpa* means cornfield, but it has also come to mean a whole system of agriculture which is still practiced in southern Mexico. Clearing the land is done by the ancient slash-and-burn technique. The trees and brush are cut and allowed to dry; the dry slash is burned, and the crop, usually beans and squash, in addition to corn, is planted just before the start of the rainy season.

These fields gradually lose their productivity, and are usually allowed to go fallow after three to five years. They are not recleared until they have lain fallow at least eight or ten years. Such a system of rotating the field, rather than crop, is practical only when there is surplus land of marginal agricultural value.

In the large areas of Mexico served by very primitive roads or by no roads at all, agriculture is, by necessity, a form of subsistence farming which participates in the economy in only a marginal way. One may see sacks of shelled corn ferried in dugout canoes for miles through mountain rapids to the nearest road-head. The heavy dugouts are then pushed laboriously back upriver, skirting the edges of the rapids, to pick up another load; two men spend two days to transport four sacks of corn ten miles. This may seem uneconomical, but seen from a sustenance point of view, it is not a bad investment. Those four large sacks of corn will provide the staple for a family of four for half a year.

Life in these back country areas sustains the traditions of Mexican cooking. The people in these remote villages often go out to find wage work in the city, and thus bring their tastes, recipes and skills to urban Mexican cuisine. They have learned to cook in a village not far away by miles, but very far away in time.

Maíz

The beginning of agriculture in the Americas probably occurred as early as 5000 B.C., parallel in time with predynastic Egypt. Pumpkins, squash, and sunflowers were among the earliest cultivated plants. But the most significant of these plants was a kind of wild *maíz* (maize in English), or corn. This plant, by a process of hybridization, became an "obligate cultivar," that is, it became totally dependent upon man. This took place so early in prehistory that the myths tell us that, "Maize was not only at the beginning . . . it was the beginning."

The origin of maize has been a subject of great speculation, of search and research. The problem with finding the ancestors of most commercial crops is that there are too many likely candidates. With corn, there are no living plants that bear that close a resemblance to the form and structure of maize.

The unique grandeur of the story of maize lies in its continuity. That the cultivation of corn persisted against all the hazards that prevailed against it, is impressive in proportion to its improbability. With pointed sticks and chipped flint points, with hoes of wood and clamshells, with no draft animal to help him, man cleared land, planted and harvested and selected his seed for the next year.

We wonder how many times this man-dependent cultivar skirted extinction when the immediate hunger of the people overwhelmed the ingrained lessons of myth and ritual that were the only protection for the precious seed corn. Not for hundreds, but for thousands of years the seeds were planted, the grass grubbed out, the suckers removed, the birds and other thieves chased away, the stalks broken over at full growth before the rains came, the dry corn shucked and the husks tied together for stringing, corn cribs built for protection from mildew and rodents — all before the seed for next season was set aside, and the labor of shelling and grinding commenced.

It isn't necessary to go back to Aztec religious myths to observe the deep reverence for corn in Mexico and the southwest U.S. It is today regarded as a "person" by the traditional Hopi; and, upon "christening," the Hopi child is given an ear of corn which becomes, from that time on, his "mother."

The widespread pre-European distribution of corn in the Americas, from near the Canadian border southward to the southern tip of Chile, allowed Indian corn to be "discovered" over and over again. The great variation in the height and growth habit of the plant and in the size, shape, and color of the grain must have caused considerable confusion. The large Peruvian corn that you may be familiar with as "Corn Nuts" is about fifty times as large as the smallest grains of popcorn. This is a much greater variation than in any other grain crop.

The North and South American Indians not only developed this astounding crop but extended its range to the geographic and climatic limits of both continents. By the advent of Europeans in the 1500's, they had already sorted out and actively cultivated all the major corn types we know today. As Paul Weatherwax says in his *Indian Corn in Old America*, "Maize is still in the process of mutation, but as far as new characteristics worth preserving are concerned, the total number we have found in four hundred years of work with the plant is negligible in comparison to what the Indian had accumulated before that."

Trucks have replaced ox carts for transport but ox teams are still important for plowing.

Fine dining in magnificent settings is found in the major cities, but village inns and markets often serve equal treats.

Rows of corn sometime appear in surprising places; here they curve along a favorite washing and swimming spot on the bank of the Rio Santiago.

It took two days to transport these sacks of shelled corn, but they will provide the basic staple for a family of four for half a year.

The Huichol Indian corn crib probably looks much the same as it did centuries ago, before the Spanish brought pigs to the scene.

Angelo Villa and his mother, Señora Maria Morales, photographed in Angelos' kitchen — "I still have to take a back seat when mother is in the kitchen."

Meet the writers and experts

The recipes in this book have been collected by Angelo Villa and Vicki Barrios. We, Marjorie and Clyde Childress, collected additional recipes in the course of photographing and interviewing in Mexico and the southwest United States.

Some of the people who shared their cooking techniques and recipes are shown on this page. We feel lucky to be able to include Angelo Villa's mother and Vicki Barrios' mother-in-law and grandmother-in-law in the group — lucky to be able to reach back a link or two in the chains that brought us these recipes.

Angelo Villa

Angelo Villa is Professor of Spanish at Valley College in Los Angeles. Professor Villa has traveled and studied in Mexico and Spain, and has lectured widely on many aspects of Hispanic culture. He is particularly expert in the history and development of Mexican cuisine.

In his words, it happened like this: "My interest in cooking started early. It happened to be Mexican cooking, since my mother was from Mexico and during part of my childhood worked as a cook.

"Some of my earliest memories go back to one of the restaurants where my mother worked. The management was proud of its food

and kitchens — and the customers, while not allowed into the kitchen, were invited to stand and watch the preparation of their food from a low partition which separated the kitchen from the dining rooms. I spent a great deal of time there as an interested spectator, but, as the son of one of the specialty cooks, I had special status. Sometimes I was honored by being allowed to go into the backyard herb garden to cut fresh cilantro, or *yerba buena* (mint) for the *albóndigas* (meat balls).

"I was fortunate in being exposed to three cultures at the same time. Typical American food was around me all the time outside my home. My mother, Maria Morales, who was born in the state of Sonora, Mexico, cooked mostly in the Mexican way. My father, on the other hand, came to this country as a young man, immigrating from Spain. Sometimes we enjoyed Spanish food at home, but it was mostly in the homes of our Spanish friends that I was introduced to the traditional foods of Spain.

"As I grew up, I discovered that everyone in Los Angeles wasn't privileged to eat as I did, and that some had never tasted and probably wouldn't even appreciate a good *enchilada* — much less a proper *machaca*. About this time, I acquired a deeper interest in the cooking and culture of ancient and modern Mexico. This interest led me eventually into my professional field of Hispanic studies. I've found that recipes and cookbooks often provide insights into a culture that one doesn't get from more formal works.

"I have tried to pass on to my own children the firm groundwork in fundamentals and the insistence on proper planning and kitchen organization that my mother gave me."

Mrs. Joseph (Noemi) Quiroga. "We use lard, beans just aren't right without it."

Doña Maria Garcia Quintero. "Just that much chocolate makes all the difference."

Señor Marcos Armas. "We make our birria in an oven; of course it's a large oven."

Mrs. Ron (Vicki) Barrios, in the center with her mother-in-law, Señora Ruth Barrios (at left) and Ruth's mother, Doña Elena Almanza — "A good cook never has a lonesome kitchen."

Vicki Barrios

Vicki Barrios teaches classes in Mexican cooking and works as a food consultant. Her interest in Mexican cooking began when she met Ron Barrios.

"When I met my husband, I knew nothing about cooking — much less Mexican cooking. My husband's parents came from different parts of Mexico, and each region has its own typical recipes. My husband's mother and grandmother lived close by, and gave me real kitchen experience."

From her mother-in-law, Vicki got an introduction to the foods of the central interior of Mexico; from Ron's grandmother, she learned the foods of the southwestern coastal region.

"Ron's parents had a grocery store in a Mexican community in Orange County in southern California; later Ron and I ran the family's second grocery.

"At first, I sort of dabbled in Mexican cooking, but pretty soon I was hooked. I worried people to distraction with my questions and devoured all the literature on Mexican cooking I could find. My appetite for the food and for information was whetted by trips to Mexico and the things that were happening in my kitchen.

"I asked my mother-in-law how I could tell when a recipe was authentic, and she replied, 'If it's cooked once, it's not Mexican.' And this I found to be pretty much true. Some dishes are boiled first, then simmered in a sauce; other dishes are fried, then baked. Even *tortillas* are cooked on a griddle, then reheated. The other test I use on a recipe is to try it out on my family. My husband has a very demanding palate. He tells me whether it is 'right' — and the children tell me whether it's good."

A book of cooks

To make a cookbook, you collect recipes and test, and collect and taste. Then, you compare and collect some more. If you are lucky, you find that you have been collecting cooks as well as recipes. We like to think of this as a book of cooks rather than a cookbook.

In these pages we are presenting real cooks, and some of the real world behind the recipes. As we remember, not one of these cooks ever said, "This is my recipe"; they were more apt to say, "The way I cook such and such is so and so; and it's pretty much the same as my mother showed me, except we like it better with more of this and less of that, which is just as well, because they don't grow much of that around here anymore."

We can't present that long chain behind each cook, but we can tell you something of how Mexican cooking became as exciting and, occasionally, as incendiary as it is today.

Dr. Roy Nakayama. "People eat a few chiles, then pretty soon they want more."

Señorita Enedina Gomez. "The vegetables aren't right unless you get to market early."

A full eight course Mexican comida with: **A.** Pico de Gallo *(Rooster's Beak, page 79)* **B.** Crema de Aguacate *(Cream of Avocado Soup, page 43)* **C.** Arroz Gualdo *(Yellow Rice, page 48)* **D.** Seviche *(Marinated Fish, page 70).*

The meal pattern in Mexico

Mexican eating patterns are different from ours. The Mexican day hinges on the *comida,* the midday dinner usually taken in early afternoon but often as late as 4 or 5 o'clock. (After all, 4 o'clock is the middle of a day that starts at 8 a.m. and ends at 12 midnight.) The timing of meals varies between city and rural dwellers, but for both, the *comida* with its *siesta* divides the day into two distinct parts, giving in effect a two-day day.

The basic meal pattern, indulged in to whatever extent individual affluence allows, starts with *desayuno,* usually coffee and *pan dulce,* upon arising, or ideally before arising. Between 10 and 11 o'clock a second breakfast follows, often more substantial, with *tortillas,* ham and eggs and chiles — this is the *almuerzo.* If you have this big, late breakfast, you are likely to take the *comida* late in the afternoon. If it is taken late enough, you are likely to make do with only one more light meal, *merienda,* which may be *café con leche* and a sweet. On special occasions there is *cena,* a light supper of two or three courses that may be served from 8 p.m. to midnight.

For some, the traditional evening meal is a soup or stew. For others, it's leftovers just as it's always been in farm homes everywhere, and it's easier to wrap a *tortilla* around leftovers than it is to balance them on a cold baking powder biscuit.

Most Americans are familiar with the typical American dinner menu of soup or salad, a main dish, one or two vegetables, dessert, and a beverage. The typical Mexican *comida* consists of an appetizer *(apertivo),* soup *(sopa),* a rice dish *(sopa seca),* a cooked vegetable or fish *(entrada),* the main course *(platillo fuerte)* usually accompanied by a salad *(ensalada),* beans *(frijoles),* dessert *(postre)* and a beverage *(bebida).*

By comparison it looks like a very heavy meal. Remember that it is taken at late midday and is intended to be lingered over. It is also followed by a *siesta.*

Such a meal in a fine restaurant can be a bit much, and the same is true when you are being entertained in an affluent private home. But in the everyday *comida* the portions served at each course are small and the total amount of food is comparable to a dinner in the U.S. The major difference is that such meals must be served in separate stages, and served while hot from the kitchen.

The cooking and serving customs in Mexico grew out of a communal way of life; each person had working responsibilities to the entire group.

Usually a number of women had the responsibility of cooking for the other members; they were able to spend their entire day preparing the *masa,* chopping, simmering and baking. Even today in Mexico, more than one woman usually manages the cooking for the family. The middleclass household has at least one woman hired full time for the kitchen. Those households of lesser means are usually an extended family, so that even if one woman is employed outside of the home, there are others at home to do the cooking and serving.

Meal planning

In the U.S., our pattern of one-cook kitchens and of busy schedules may seem to limit the feasibility of preparing authentic Mexican foods. Although none of the techniques involved in Mexican cooking is difficult, you may at first find them time-consuming. Therefore, rather than tackle a full-course Mexican meal, begin by first replacing one or two items in your meal with Mexican dishes. As a start you might try the *chile verde* (page 57) or *enchiladas* (pages 35 to 36) accompanied by your favorite green salad.

Serve a *sopa seca* (page 48 to 49) with your next pot roast, or a marinated zucchini salad (page 78)

E. Pollo Almendrado *(Almond Chicken, page 66)* *F.* Frijoles de Olla *(Beans from the Pot, page 78)*
G. Chayote Relleno *(Filled Chayote, page 88)* *H.* Cafe con Leche *(Coffee with Milk, page 92).*

with grilled salmon, or *nopales* salad (page 81) with a barbecued steak.

When you feel ready to put together a "Mexican only" meal, don't try to go full course the first time. A main dish, salad, rice or beans accompanied by *tortillas* and butter, is a good meal.

Although we don't really like to recommend it, you can also pad out an authentic main course with a simple Mexican style soup: a clear, canned chicken broth with chopped onions, with slices of avocado floating on top and a wedge of lime on the side. Put a dish of ready prepared *salsa* (sauce) on the table and serve fresh fruit for dessert.

The following menus allow you to start off with family meals of one or two Mexican recipes. (Boldface type indicates that the recipe is included in this book.)

Family menu I

Start simply with a Mexican dish as a main course:

Chile Verde (Pork and Green Chile Stew), page 57
Arroz Blanco (White Rice), page 49
Add your favorite green salad and a dessert to complete the meal.

Family menu II

A second family menu has three Mexican dishes:

Enchiladas (Beef or Chicken), pages 35 to 36

Frijoles Refritos (Well-fried Beans) page 78
Ensalada de Calabacitas (Zucchini Salad), page 78

Family menu III

This menu is designed to work as a light evening meal or a hearty weekend lunch.

Sopa de Albóndigas (Meatball Soup), page 46
Hot **tortillas** with butter
Mexican beer
Fresh fruit for dessert.

Family menu IV

Now begin to expand. Add a soup course to begin the meal, a dessert, after-dinner coffee and, to complete the meal . . . invite guests.

Sopa de Aguacate (Avocado Soup), page 43
Huachinango a la Veracruzana (Red Snapper Vera Cruz Style), page 69
Ejotes y Papas (Green Beans and Potatoes), page 76
Hard crust rolls or French bread and butter
Flan (Custard), page 83
Café de Olla (Coffee), page 92

The Mexican brunch

Papaya, cut into quarters and served with lime wedges
Chilaquiles *(Tortilla* Casserole), using egg variation, page 41, or
Huevos Rancheros (Ranch-Style Eggs), page 66

Frijoles Refritos (Well-fried Beans), page 78
Pan Dulce (Sweet Rolls), page 87
Chocolate Mexicano (Mexican Chocolate), page 92

Summer evening buffet

This entire meal is prepared in advance and served chilled.

Sopa de Melón Escribe (Chilled Cantaloupe Soup), page 43
Fiambres Surtidos (Assorted Cold Meats and Vegetables), page 59
Garnishes to accompany the **Fiambres Surtidos,** page 60
Bolillos (French rolls)
Mexican beer
Café de Olla (Coffee), page 92
Helado de Mango (Mango Ice), page 83

Holiday meal

Mole Poblano (Chicken in Mole), page 63
Tamales Blancos (White Tamales), page 41, or
Arroz Blanco (White Rice), page 51
Ensalada de Noche Buena (Christmas Eve Salad), page 79, or
Fresh fruit or melon
Chayotes Rellenos (Stuffed Chayotes), page 88
Café de Olla (Coffee), page 92

When preparing Mexican recipes, make more than you need for one meal and freeze it. The next time you get hungry at 4 o'clock, you can have a Mexican meal at 6 o'clock.

On weekends and holidays . . .

in the parks and public places . . .

you are seldom out of reach . . .

How Mexico snacks

Eating in Mexico is both a celebration and a sacrament. For Mexicans, food and fiesta minister to deep human needs that we often seem too ready to surrender to the instant low calorie lunch.

All of mankind's food must have started as finger food and new finger snacks seem to appear in our markets almost daily; after all, knives and forks at the table are a rather recent innovation. The Mexican system of finger food must be a high point in variety and sophistication. We can assume that Montezuma and Cortés both ate with their fingers, but the *tortilla* gave Montezuma a neat advantage.

Food vendors and eaters

The ancient Mexicans also impaled their food on sticks (as we all still do) and used hollow quills as drinking straws. They would still feel right at home with the food shown here.

To spend a Sunday at a Mexican public park or beach, observing the food sellers and joining the eaters, can be a very special holiday. Appetite and appreciation are contagious.

On market day in the villages, in the open-air markets of the cities — wherever people gather — the food sellers are on hand. The more mobile vendors tour the neighborhood on regular routes, pausing where the crowds gather.

At Los Muertos beach in Puerto

Vallarta where these photographs were taken, there are open-air restaurants and bars, as well as vendors, and the range of edibles runs from a full *comida* at top tourist prices to a cup of sweetened rice for a peso.

If you can't find an empty *palapa* (a palm thatched shade) on the beach, you can lie on your beach towels, or rent chairs and woven mats from a small boy who immediately materializes at your elbow.

Now you can settle down with your choice of either sun or shade. And just as quickly the vending parade begins: beer and soft drinks, delicious fish tidbits on a stick, juicy mangoes, peeled, serrated (also impaled on a stick), watermelon (ready with a square of paper to hold

and buy from the vendors or . . .

wander down the beach for coconuts, . . .

barbecued sierra and Pacific snapper, or . . .

of great finger food.

At Los Muertos beach at Puerto Vallarta,

you can stay in the shade . . .

it) and all manner of *licuados* (fruit drinks).

The vendors never seem to push, and on occasion it appears they would just as soon keep their fare for supper as sell it to you.

There are snacks for all hours of the day and all the moods of celebration: fruit and ices and melon and pineapple and green coconuts with the top hacked off for straws to reach the sweet-flavored milk. Fish seems to span the entire day since it is a "cool" food, even when hot from the charcoal grill.

In the folk tradition of Mexican cooking, food is classified as either hot or cold in a manner quite similar to the tradition in Chinese cooking. This classification has little or nothing to do with the temperature of the food, but rather with the effect of the food on the body. Hot foods are those that digest easily and produce heat in the body, while cold foods are difficult to digest and lower body heat. According to Francis Toor in the book *Mexican Folkways,* some foods considered hot are: coffee, beef, honey and *pinole,* while pork, rice, boiled eggs, papaya, limes and squash are cold. Many foods — chicken, oranges, tomatoes, beans and tortillas — are simply medium. Proper balance of hot and cold foods is considered necessary to good health.

We happened to be in Puerto Vallarta on *Día de Niños* (Children's Day), so after the beach we went to the evening celebration at the amphi-

theatre by the bay. There was a program of music, speeches and folkdancing.

Before the celebration, we ate *seviche* (marinated fish) bought from the lady at the post office corner. Then after watching all the dancing and eating, we walked along the bay on the *malecón.* Feeling hungry again, we bought *elotes,* young ears of sweet corn, neatly impaled on a stick, dipped in heavy sweet cream and sprinkled liberally with grated *queso añejo,* a nice, sharp crumbly cheese.

We couldn't help wondering what the people who had eaten a full meal at noon were doing. We suspect that they had learned to pace themselves better than we had.

mangoes, melons, papayas and jícama or, . . . corn coated with cream and grated cheese. Dozens of treats to fill you and your day.

Mexican kitchen

The Mexican kitchen of today is a combination — a blending of the best pre-Hispanic practices and ingredients, with much of the best that Europe could offer.

Pre-Hispanic Mexico was wealthy in food resources, fully as rich as the Old World: many kinds of corn, chocolate, peanuts, pumpkins, tomatoes, pineapple, potatoes, dozens of different beans, chiles, papaya, avocado, sweet potato, sunflower, *chayote, jícama, nopales,* vanilla — all of these now more or less familiar to us — and dozens of others that haven't yet found favor beyond their own regions. When we read the list of food, it doesn't seem to need much addition; yet the people of Mexico must have been just as interested in the new foods the Spanish brought as the Europeans were in the wealth of new plants sent back to Europe.

The Mexican colonial kitchen combined most of the best ingredients of the old and new worlds, and the tools and techniques as well. There was a standup stove, if not always a chimney to go with it. And the beehive oven was there for baking bread. Animal power was used to grind the wheat that became common in the north, and to grind the sugar cane that was made into heavy syrup or solid *piloncillos.* Of course there was still the kneel-down *metate* for grinding *masa* (corn dough). Better ways of doing this were still a long way off.

Among all that the Spanish brought to Mexico, the most immediate and most profound changes were caused by the livestock. (The only pre-Hispanic domesticated animals were the dog and the turkey.) The horse

◁

The center column in Señora María Asunción Sánchez's kitchen in San Sebastian is the chimney: the free-standing stove extends around three sides. There is also a gas stove but it "just doesn't do everything."

had an immediate super-weapon effect, instilling fear in the Indian warriors. It was a pivotal factor in Cortés' first military campaigns. But of all the Spanish introductions, the pig was the catalyst for the greatest changes in the kitchen. It wasn't the meat, popular as it must have been. It was the lard, and the availability of fat for frying.

It would be a mistake to assume that the blending of Indian and European methods is now complete.

Co-author Vicki Barrios' mother-in-law said, "It isn't Mexican if it's only cooked once." Of course this isn't always true, but it probably is true that Mexican cooking has more than its share of re-cooked dishes. Part of this may be due simply to the way the *tortilla* lends itself to multiple use and recycling. However, if we look at the number of times that an ingredient is either boiled or dry-cooked first and then fried and baked, it seems plausible to suggest that many dishes are cooked in an Indian style first and Spanish second.

Though traditional Mexican cooking is often laborious and generally time consuming, there are short cuts. These may not always give you complete authenticity, but we will recommend those we've tried and found satisfactory.

Household tools

Many kitchens in Mexico are still equipped with most of the household tools of pre-Conquest Mexico: the *metate* and *mano, molcajete, molinillo, cazuelas* and *ollas.* In the country kitchens, these may still be the primary tools; but in the fine kitchens of the city, they may be primarily decorative. The *metate* and *mano* (grinding stone) have been largely outmoded

by store-bought *masa.* But in many kitchens they still sit on a ledge about a foot below counter height, so that you can get your back into the work. They are still used to "silken" the store-bought *masa* just before it's balled and patted and flattened in the press and they are often more convenient for grinding nuts and puréeing tomatoes than the blender sitting beside them. As useful as the traditional tools once were, and still are to those apprenticed in their use, most of those you buy are likely to become kitchen and table decorations. If you get serious about Mexican cooking, a *tortilla* press may become indispensible and a good *molcajete* (after you have ground away all the loose grit) may work a bit better than your mortar and pestle.

You will need a good blender or food processor, and a small electric coffee grinder with a sharp blade is handy for making powdered chile, grinding chile seeds, nuts and fresh roasted Mexican coffee beans.

The metate *is still used to silken the* masa, *even when it is bought from the store already ground.*

1. Ollas *(deep cooking pots)* **2.** Olla para frijoles *(special pot for beans)* **3.** Charcoal grill *(made from a 5 gallon oil can)* **4.** Molcajete y tejolote *(mortar and pestle)* **5.** Metate y Mano *(flat stone grinder and muller for grinding corn)* **6.** Tortilla press *(common aluminum type)* **7.** Cazuelas *(pottery casseroles)* **8.** Nested cooking dishes **9.** Molinillo *(carved chocolate beater)* **10.** Bean masher **11.** Lime juicer **12.** Comal *(thick iron griddle).*

Ingredients

Most of the ingredients you will need to cook the recipes in this book are probably familiar to you, but some are used so differently that it may be just as well to talk about them as if you had never heard of them. There are a few ingredients that you are likely to find only in Latin American groceries, but you can grow a number of them in your own garden. See page 19.

To appreciate the logic and beauty of Mexican cooking, we need to learn as much as we can about Indian corn, and acquaint ourselves with the versatile chiles. For these reasons and because we know many of you are interested in gardening, we will devote more extensive sections to these two crops. (See pages 4 and 21.)

Achiote
(Seeds for flavoring and coloring)

Achiote is Spanish for the seed of the annatto tree *(Bixa orellana).* The seeds are deep red-orange and used for the brilliant yellow color they impart to other food, as well as for their subtle flavor. The dried seeds are cooked in lard or oil until the lard is well colored, then the seeds are removed. See recipe for yellow rice (page 48).

A powder, made from the seeds, is used for tinting many things, including butter.

In Yucatán, *achiote* seeds are ground into a paste and used as a base to season meat and fish. The seeds can be found in markets specializing in Latin American foods.

Aguacate
(Avocado)

Avocados are shipped to market unripened and, often, as hard as rocks. They ripen quickly — within two or three days — in a warm kitchen or on a sunny windowsill.

Properly ripe and ready to use, avocados should be soft but not mushy, and the seed shouldn't rattle when you shake the fruit. The texture of the flesh should be firm and buttery. There are several varieties, but you'll probably find either the large, smooth-skinned green ones or the smaller, bumpy skinned black ones. The black ones are the best. These are the Hass variety, and available only in the summer. In the winter, there is a number of different smooth-skinned varieties available; the Fuerte is excellent. Unfortunately most of the others are grown primarily because they ripen early and bear heavily, but they are often watery and rather flavorless. The Fuerte can be distinguished from these less desirable avocados since it has a less glossy appearance. If in doubt, ask your produce man at the market.

Leaves can be used fresh or dried, ground or whole. They are usually toasted lightly first to bring out the flavor. To find out how strong the flavor of the leaves is, crumble one roughly in your hand or grind it to a powder. It should have the slightly licorice smell of a ripe avocado.

Camarón Seco
(Dried shrimp)

Dried shrimp are available either shredded or whole with the heads and tails already removed. Toasting them lightly until they are crisp improves the flavor. Toast in a low oven, or in a dry frying pan on top of the stove.

Canela
(Cinnamon)

Both true cinnamon bark and cassia bark are sold as cinnamon in the U.S.

In Mexico, true cinnamon is highly esteemed, and almost all of the true cinnamon imported into the U.S. is re-exported to Mexico. True cinnamon is more delicate in flavor and generally sold in thin quills. In powdered form, true cinnamon is more of a tan color, compared to the reddish brown color of cassia.

Cebollas
(Onions)

Find a white onion variety with a good sharp bite to it. White onions are very important for salads, table *salsas,* and fish recipes. Where there's a significant price difference, yellow onions can substitute in dishes other than those listed above. In general, the yellow onions are too sweet. Purple onions are served pickled and as garnishes for *antojitos,* but they don't have the necessary bite when cooked.

Chayote
(Vegetable pear or christophine)

This member of the squash family is unlike any other in appearance, texture, or taste. It is becoming increasingly available in better markets here. Its subtle texture has made it popular in Chinese cooking, so it is almost always available in Chinese as well as Latin markets.

We find it difficult to explain why *chayote* is such an elegant vegetable, since it doesn't have any spectacular attributes. Its flesh has a reticulated texture like a pear or a watermelon, only much more delicate. The flavor is a bit like cucumber, but much more subtle. Large *chayotes* should be cut in half or quartered before cooking, and the edible seed should be cut and cooked with it.

It is best appreciated in simple form: boiled, peeled, and served hot with butter, or cold in a salad. It is excellent in soups, such as the chicken soup on page 44, where the texture and flavor of each ingredient is appreciated separately.

Chiles
See page 21.

Chorizo
(Sausage)
Chorizo is a highly seasoned, coarsely ground pork sausage, usually in links. The Mexican *chorizo* is made with fresh pork; the Spanish version is made with smoked pork.

Always remove the casing before cooking, and break the sausage meat apart slightly. It must be cooked thoroughly.

Cilantro
(Fresh coriander, Chinese parsley)
Fresh coriander is called *cilantro* by the Mexicans, *cilantrillo* by Puerto Ricans, and Chinese parsley by many Americans. In Mexican cooking, the fresh leaves of the plant are used. *Cilantro* has a very distinctive flavor and should be used carefully until you find out how well you like it.

Don't try to substitute the easily available coriander seeds for the fresh leaf; its flavor is entirely different. Ground coriander seed is used in several recipes in this book.

Buy *cilantro* with the roots still on at Oriental or Mexican markets if your local supermarket doesn't have it. To store, refrigerate it unwashed with the roots in a glass of water and covered with a plastic bag. Wash it just before you use it. It doesn't freeze well and there is no substitute.

Epazote
(*Chenopodium,* Lamb's quarters)
The *epazote* of central Mexico has an odor that takes some getting used to. It is considered a must for flavoring black beans and is used with a number of other foods. *Chenopodiums* are frequently used as pot herbs in

Europe and the U.S. These were once cultivated plants and may now be found wild in much of the country. They are generally identified as lamb's quarters and are less strong in flavor than the Mexican *epazote*. The strong Mexican variety is *Chenopodium ambrosioides;* the common milder ones are probably *C. fremontii* and *C. album*.

Besides being a nutritious green, *epazotes* are known as carminatives and used to reduce the gas associated with beans. As we were told once in New Mexico, "The only thing for beans is *epazote*." Just how seriously we should take this claim should be viewed in the light of the number of other herbs and spices that are said to be carminatives: oregano, mint, cumin, rosemary, anise and, of course, chiles.

Epazote is used as a seasoning as well as a pot herb. The amount you use for seasoning will vary with the strength of the herb; older plants are more suitable for seasoning, younger ones for greens.

Frijoles
(Beans)
Beans are used in such great variety in Mexico that one sometimes

wonders whether the color of the displays in the market may not be as much a reason for their presence as the range of flavors and cooking characteristics. They come in black and white and in yellows, reds, pinks and purples. Varieties include *frijol negro, haba, azufrado, vallarta, canario* and the brightly speckled *flor de mayo,* the "may flower," a name as pretty as the bean.

In the large city markets, each bean merchant will display baskets with as many as fifteen or twenty varieties. Rural markets will often have only half as many — depending on the differences in regional preferences.

Your own selection of beans at your local market is likely to include pinto, pink, red, black, kidney and white.

In Mexico, soaking beans overnight is considered unnecessary and undesirable. They should be cooked slowly with nothing more than water, lard, and salt which is added only after the beans are soft — except in pressure cooked beans (page 78). Cooked beans improve in flavor after a day or two, but should be refrigerated.

Fifteen or twenty different varieties of beans are offered in markets like this one in Guadalajara. No one cook is likely to need so many, but each cook wants the right one — and the right one differs if you are from Chiapas or from Chihuahua.

In this village market, the glass case holds wheels of queso fresco *(fresh cheese)* *and is surrounded by garlic, chiles, onions, beans and* chayotes.

Hojas
(Corn husks)

Corn husks are the traditional wrapping for *tamales.* They're available dried and packaged in Mexican markets and in the specialty section of supermarkets. They are ready to use when flattened with the ends trimmed. If you get some in their natural state, cut off the butt end to make them straight and even.

To soften the corn husks for use, put them in a deep pan, pour very hot water over them, and leave them to soak for several hours. When you're ready to use them, drain or shake to get rid of the excess water and pat them dry with paper towels. They'll be flexible enough to fill, wrap, and tie for the tamales. The ties are made by tearing some of the corn husks into strips.

Jícama
(Root vegetable)

Jícama is a sweet, brown, round root vegetable, white on the inside, which has a crisp texture retained even after cooking. Use it raw or sauté it lightly; it's rather like water chestnuts.

Lard
(Cooking fats and oils)

The introduction of the pig to Mexico signaled the only truly basic change in the ancient cooking system. Lard from the pig is still the preferred cooking fat. A friend, Noemi Quiroga, told us as she worked the lard into her flour, "After all this business of cholesterol, you know we were raised on lard — beans just don't taste good with shortening, vegetable oil, or anything like that. And your flour *tortillas,* you just don't make them with shortening. It's just not heard of."

We, too, had never doubted the importance of lard as a flavor enhancing cooking oil until we participated in some taste tests with lard versus vegetable shortening in refried beans. Now we're not so confident about the importance of lard. As it turned out, we could tell the difference, but it took awhile to be certain. If you are worried about saturated fats, go right ahead and substitute low cholesterol vegetable oil.

The distinctive flavor of lard and some other oils is subdued by "burning" the lard or oil before frying, that is, heating it until it barely begins to smoke, or bubbles rapidly around a wooden spoon. Allow it to cool a little, then add the food.

Commercial lard is readily available. But if you find yourself with a surplus of pork fat, here's how you can make your own.

1. Chop pork fat into small pieces.

2. Put in a large heavy pot over low heat. Stir often to keep the cracklings from sticking and scorching. As the water in the fat evaporates, the temperature will rise. Use a deep fat thermometer to make sure the temperature doesn't go above 255 degrees F. Continue cooking slowly,

Epazote *is a favored* quelite *(spring green), as well as an important seasoning herb, particularly for beans.*

until the fat is thoroughly rendered (to 255 degrees), otherwise moisture may be left that can cause the lard to sour.

3. Let cool, until comfortable to handle. Dip off the lard at the top of the pot, put into a clean container, strain and add the rest. Save the crackling.

4. Store in a cool place.

Preserving lard or oil for reuse: Strain through 4 layers of cheesecloth into a clean glass jar. Keep refrigerated. If the oil becomes cloudy after several uses, place 3 parts water to 1 part oil in a large pot. Boil 10 minutes. The mixture will boil at the boiling point of water, preventing the oil from splattering or popping. Refrigerate overnight. Water will carry residue to bottom. Skim the oil from surface and strain into a clean glass jar. Keep refrigerated.

Maíz
(Corn)
See page 4, and page 29 for *Masa*.

Nopales
(Cactus sections)
These are the thick, elliptical paddles or "leaves" of several varieties of prickly pear cactus (*Opuntia*). If you can find them fresh, choose the smallest, thinnest, palest ones — they'll be the most tender and the best flavored. It's rather like selecting young asparagus.

Some *Opuntia* varieties are spineless, but if you get the thorny kind, you'll have to scrape off the cactus spines from the sides and edges. Use tongs to handle; the spines are nasty. Leave as much of the green skin as possible. Cut into small pieces, and cook until tender in well-salted water.

Cooked *nopales* may have a slippery quality somewhat like okra. There are several ways to minimize this. After cooking, rinse and drain in a colander, cover with a damp towel to keep them from drying out, and let stand for about 30 minutes. Another way is to cook diced *nopales* a few minutes in an ungreased pan with several chunks of onion and a clove or two of garlic until the slippery materials come out. Rinse in a colander, then proceed with the recipe.

If you can't find fresh ones, the canned *nopales* are a good substitute. Pickled *nopales (en escabeche)* are also available.

Nueces y Semillas
(Nuts and seeds)
Peanuts, pecans and pumpkin seeds are all native to Mexico. They are ground very fine and are often used instead of flour, egg yolks or cream to thicken sauces.

The Spanish introduced almonds, filberts, walnuts, pine nuts and sesame seeds, widely used throughout Mexico and all are readily available in the U.S.

Pumpkin seeds (*pepitas*) are ground and used as a base for sauces. Look for the shelled, unsalted ones in health food stores or specialty shops.

Oregano
(Fresh or dried herb)
In Mexico there are many different plants called oregano. The favored Mexican oregano is a small shrub of the *Verbena* family. It is more aromatic and pungent than the Mediterranean *Originam* species.

Oregano is often combined in Mexican cooking with cumin and cloves as a seasoning trio. The classically balanced ratio for these three is twice as much oregano as cumin, twice as much cumin as cloves. For example, ½ teaspoon oregano. ¼ teaspoon cumin, ⅛ teaspoon cloves is a good balance, based on normal strength for each of the flavors.

Piloncillo
(Raw sugar cones)
Piloncillo is Mexican raw sugar sold in very small to very large cones. Dark brown sugar may be substituted.

Plátano macho
(Plantains, cooking bananas)
Plantains are a large banana variety which must be cooked to be edible. They must also be ripe to be peeled; ripe ones are both black and soft. The most common way to cook them is to slice them lengthwise ½ inch thick and fry them in oil. Another way is to slice them into thin rounds and fry until crisp — they taste like potato chips, but sweet. Regular green, firm bananas will substitute, but they need less cooking time.

Queso
(Cheese)
Since the Spanish introduction of cows and goats in the sixteenth century, cheese has become an integral element of Mexican cooking. Dozens of varieties have been developed for stuffing, layering and garnishing.

Besides adding distinctive tastes and textures to dishes, cheese stores surplus milk, containing nearly all the fat, casein, calcium, and vitamin A that was in the milk. Cheese is about 25 percent casein, a valuable protein which constitutes only 3 per cent of whole milk. As an important bonus, cheese nicely complements the

Mexican oregano, (or Mexican sage) is a member of the Verbena *family.*

Dried seasoning herbs are sometimes sold along with herbal medicinals.

Yes, those are bananas, but would you recognize the others as potatoes?

relatively incomplete proteins found in beans and corn, making them nutritionally more valuable.

Good Mexican cheeses are rarely available in the United States. If you have no luck at the Mexican markets, and you're the do-it-yourself type, try making your own cheeses. (See the Ortho book *12 Months Harvest.*) Or, try the following substitutions.

Queso fresco: a fresh, unripened, perishable cheese. Substitute dry cottage cheese or Italian ricotta. If these seem too mild, try mixing them with a little Greek feta cheese, or make your own whey cheese.

Queso panela: a mild cheese, aged in baskets, and therefore readily identified by the woven markings on the rind. Substitute Monterey jack.

Queso añejo: sharp and salty. Try using Gruyere; excellent for filling enchiladas.

Queso Chihuahua: also sharp, but softer and less salty than *queso añejo.* Medium cheddar, Parmesan, or Romano make fair substitutes.

Queso de Oaxaca: stringy and slightly tart. Use Monterey jack.

Queso asadero: a mild cheese, comes thinly sliced and packaged like *tortillas.* Substitute provolone or mozzarella.

Tomate, jitomate
(Tomatoes)

American tomatoes have been bred for their shipping qualities, unfortunately, at the expense of flavor. They are often gas ripened rather than vine ripened. If such tomatoes are all that's available, opt for canned ones. For best flavor, grow your own.

Tomatoes are often *asado* (roasted) in Mexican recipes. This is traditionally done on the *comal,* but it's messy. It's easier to line a shallow pan with aluminum foil and slip the tomatoes under the broiler for 20 minutes for a medium-sized tomato. Turn to cook evenly. The skin may be removed or left on but the charred skin adds flavor. Blend into a fairly smooth sauce.

To peel tomatoes, dip them in boiling water for a minute or two. The skin will slip off easily.

Tomatillo
(Also called *tomate de cascara*)

There are a number of similar plants, both wild and cultivated, in this group that are often seen in Mexican markets. These vary from the size of a large pea to the size of a golf ball. The smaller varieties resemble our husk tomato, (ground cherry, or cape

In the 2,000 stalls of the Mercado Libertad in Guadalajara you will find the fresh produce of all Mexico; as well as hundreds of food stands and sit-down restaurants serving an incredible variety of prepared food. All this, plus hardware, clothing, jewelry, two banks, a police station, even a public school on the roof.

gooseberry), but the real *tomatillo (Physalis ixocarpa)* generally fills the paper-like husk, rather than hanging within it as most of the others do.

This is a cooking vegetable and does not develop its best flavor until cooked .They are available canned, called *tomatillos entero* or *tomate verde.*

Two basic cooking methods for preparation of fresh *tomatillos:*

1. Remove the husk and rinse the *tomatillos.* Place in a saucepan and cover with cold water. Bring to a boil and cook over low heat for approximately 5 minutes, until transparent. Drain, to use immediately, or store in the refrigerator or freezer in their own liquid.

2. Pre-heat the *comal* or heavy frying pan over medium heat. Place the *tomatillos* on the *comal* with their husks on. Toast gently, turning often, until the *tomatillo* flesh is soft and the husk quite brown (approximately 10 minutes). Remove husk.

Your own Mexican garden

Some of the vegetables and herbs that are important in the Mexican kitchen are not available in parts of the U.S. But if you garden you can get seeds for most of these and grow your own.

The most important plants that could be difficult to obtain are: The *tomatillo* (or *tomate verde*), *cilantro* (coriander) and an adequate selection of chile varieties. All these can be raised successfully in most of the country and seeds are easily available.

There is a good chance that *epazote* (chenopodium, goosefoot, lamb's quarters) already grows wild in your area, even though it may not be the strong Mexican *Chenopodium ambrosioides*. Seeds for it are available and it's easy to grow. You may also have *yerba buena,* or spearmint, growing in your garden, if not get a start from a neighbor, or your nurseryman.

Real Mexican wild oregano will be hard to find unless you live in the southwest and can find it growing wild, but the usual oregano or wild marjoram *(Origanum vulgare)* is quite adequate.

Avocado

If you wish to use avocado leaves as a seasoning, save the seed from your market fruit. Plant it broad end down in a small pot of soil or suspended in a glass of water. After a very long time (sometimes as long as six months) it will sprout and then grow quickly into a small, handsome plant. We often place a half-dozen seeds in an eight-inch pot and grow a small forest so that when we use the leaves in cooking, no one plant gets stripped. The flavor is stronger when the avocado is grown outside and leaves are mature, so, if yours is a house plant, use at least twice as many leaves.

Chayote

(Vegetable pear)
The *chayote* is a member of the gourd family but certainly doesn't look like a gourd. It grows as a perennial in mild-winter areas. Frost will kill the tops back each winter but the vine renews itself in spring. It is a fast-growing vine and is best handled on a trellis or fence. It flowers in late summer and fruit is harvested about a month later, continuing until it is stopped by frost. In cold climates use a deep winter mulch — 10 inches or more of compost — pull it aside at sprouting time in the spring.

Use a whole fruit as seed, planted with the large end sloping downward in the soil and the small end slightly exposed. Go easy on watering at the start; overwatering can cause the seed to rot.

Chiles

The most useful chile selection you can grow will include at least one of the large mild cooking chiles, either the broad *ancho, mulato* or the long green Anaheim, or mild New Mexico chile. You will also need one or two of the small garnish chiles — more if you like to experiment and really want to find the right chiles for your climate.

Chiles are generally classified as hot weather vegetables but heat requirements are not as high as you might suppose. If night temperatures go much below 60 degrees or above 75 degrees the plants will get blossom drop. Daytime temperatures above 90 degrees also cause blossom drop, but plants will resume fruit setting with the return of lower temperatures.

A good selection for most areas would be the Anaheim or the College 6-4 for a mild cooking chile. Choose the *jalapeño* and Fresno for garnish chiles. (The Fresno makes a handsome ornamental pot plant.) The Hungarian hot wax chile and the long red cayenne are good selections that mature early and extend the growing range.

When you pick your own green chiles. Green chiles to be used fresh should be picked when mature but before they begin to turn red. If they are picked too early they will not have developed their full flavor. You can identify a mature green chile by its appearance, feel and sound but all the criteria are rather subtle, or at least difficult to explain. A mature chile becomes slightly less glossy than an immature one; if you press it gently and roll slightly between the fingers, you can feel the placental membrane inside the chile release from the outer shell with a slight snapping or squeaking sound.

Good sources for seeds are: Horticultural Enterprises, P.O. Box 34082, Dallas, Texas 75234 and The Rocky Mountain Seed Co., 1321-27 Fifteenth St., P.O. Box 5204, Denver, Colorado 80217.

Cilantro

(Coriander, Chinese parsley)
This fast-growing annual reaches a height of 1 to 2 feet. It is easy to grow and may be planted in place and thinned 6 or 7 inches apart. You can sow the whole coriander seeds you buy as a spice. The seeds should be sown ¼-inch deep in rows about 6 inches apart. They usually take about 2 weeks to sprout. Pick young sprigs as you would parsley.

Seeds can be obtained (as coriander) from Nichols Garden Nursery, 1190 North Pacific Hwy., Albany, Oregon 97321.

Epazote

(Chenopodium, Lambs quarters)
This leggy plant with narrow serrated leaves hardly needs cultivation; once started it will take care of itself in back corners of the garden. It seems to develop its best flavoring qualities when grown under stress. The fresh well-watered spring growth is bland enough for a pot herb.

Seeds can be obtained from Horticultural Enterprises, P.O. Box 34082, Dallas, Texas 75234.

Jícama

If you live where the growing season is long and hot, *jícama* is easily grown. Plant seeds in early spring when the soil is warm. It will become a large, white-flowered vine. Soil should be loose and well-worked. Mulching is beneficial.

Seed can be obtained from Horticultural Enterprises, (see address above), or from Gurney Seed and Nursery Co., Yankton, South Dakota 57079.

Tomatillo

The culture of the tart-fruited *tomatillo* is essentially the same as the tomato. Seed sown in peat pots will germinate in about 5 days and be ready to transplant in 2 to 3 weeks.

Tomatillos used for cooking are harvested as needed, but must be harvested as soon as husks turn from green to tan, otherwise they lose their tartness and become soft. *Tomatillos* in their husks can be stored for months if placed in a cool, well-ventilated location.

You may save seed from market fruit or they can be obtained from Horticultural Enterprises.

Chiles and salsas

The idea that a lot of chiles are used in Mexican cooking is true. The idea that all chile-flavored foods are "red hot" is not true. The chile is a versatile ingredient with a great range of uses and flavors.

In learning to prepare Mexican food, the cook must, very early, face up to the chile. One of the first comments we should make to the tender-mouthed readers who can't eat hot chiles is to reassure you that you don't have to know all about chiles to do some pretty fancy Mexican cooking. Still, it just isn't possible to skip lightly over the one item that emphatically says "Mexican" to most people.

The chile is a member of the genus *Capsicum* and is unrelated to the *Piper* family from which we get black pepper; it is, therefore, illogical to speak of "chile pepper."

Even in the notoriously non-standardized field of recipe writing — where a pinch is still a measurement, and a heaping teaspoon a precise measurement — the chile is a moving target that defies standardization.

A beginning Mexican cook will want to know which chiles are hot and which ones are less severe. Our illustrations on page 22-23 break the chiles into hot and mild groups, but you will discover you have to taste the chiles to find your preferences.

Part of the chile problem is that there are many varieties (probably over one hundred in Mexico), and all of these cross-pollinate with great ease. As if this weren't enough, a chile which is mild when grown in the happy conditions of a California coastal valley will become a "hot" chile when grown in the sterner, more stressful conditions of New Mexico.

◁

Ristras of chiles hang on an adobe wall in Chimayo, New Mexico. Each ristra *was 2 bushels of chiles before drying.*

Despite our earlier reassurance, there's no denying the fact that chile is omnipresent in Mexico as a *salsa.* There are some Mexican dishes truly built upon chile, such as *moles, adobos,* and *chiles rellenos.* But even these can generally be made with chiles mild enough to suit all but the most delicate palates.

The next thing we must emphasize is that chiles are good for you — possibly in more ways than you have ever imagined. They are an excellent source of vitamin A (carotene) and vitamin C (ascorbic acid).

The vitamin A is largely retained even when the chile is canned, frozen or dried. The vitamin C increases in green chiles through the growing season and peaks just before the pods turn red. About two-thirds of the vitamin C is retained in canned and frozen chiles — but dried chiles lose their vitamin C. The bright red and yellow color of ripe chiles is due to the content of capsanthin and various other carotenoids including carotene (vitamin A). More than half the commercial chile crop ends up as coloring for food and cosmetics. The "hot" or pungent principle, is called capsaicin. It is concentrated in the cental ribs and veins where the seeds attach.

The effect of chiles on the digestion is likely to play a major part in any spirited chile discussion. Very early medical literature in western Europe was likely to ascribe rather miraculous efficacy to chile. It was touted as a cure for many ailments from dropsy, colic and diarrhea to toothache and constipation.

During the early years of scientific nutritional research in the U.S., the chile was either dismissed as a crude way of adding a bit of flair

to the monotonous diet of the tropics, to "take poverty off the minds of the poor." It was more firmly condemned as a means of concealing the flavor of rotten meat. In 1924, a book on Mexico concluded, "The most detrimental factor in the (Mexican) diet is the caustic chile."

It might now be worthwhile to examine some of the medicinal attributes of chiles as they look after a few more years of research. Besides the vitamins that are present in important quantities, we know that the chile, as an aid to digestion, increases salivation (as much as eight times above the normal resting rate). Taken internally, chiles can raise body temperature and act as a general stimulant. Externally, they act as a counter-irritant for relief of muscular pain.

One of the most significant recent findings suggests that the early Indians knew what they were doing when they coated their meats with chile pulp. Studies at New Mexico State University show that chile is an antioxidant and when

The soft ingredients for salsas *are quickly blended on the* metate.

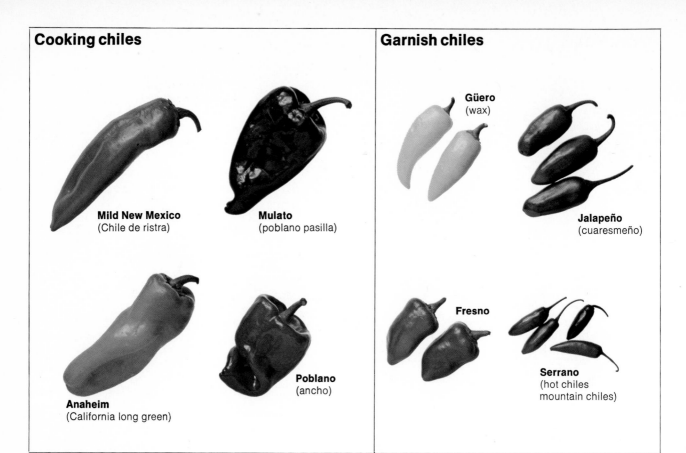

Cooking chiles

Mild New Mexico
(Chile de ristra)

Mulato
(poblano pasilla)

Anaheim
(California long green)

Poblano
(ancho)

Garnish chiles

Güero
(wax)

Jalapeño
(cuaresmeño)

Fresno

Serrano
(hot chiles
mountain chiles)

---

included in meat dishes it retards the oxidization of fats, delays rancidity and contributes to significantly longer storage life.

In Mexico, chiles are commonly named by their use, such as *chile para relleno* (for stuffing) or *huachinango* (to be cooked with red snapper), or they may be named for a region such as Tabasco, or the shape of the chile such as *ancho* (broad), or its color, *güero* (blond) or *colorado* (red). In most cases, the name changes when the chile is dried. In addition, the name *pasilla* is confusingly applied to six or seven different dried *or* fresh chiles, most of them mild.

Dr. Roy Nakayama of the New Mexico State University horticulture department (known as the "Doctor of Hot" among some chile aficionados) told us of ordering *pasillas* from as many different sources as he could find. The seeds from these gave him plants that varied all the way from long slender shapes to full, broad *ancho* types.

Dr. Nakayama and his associates at New Mexico State University developed the New Mexico 6-4, mildest of the New Mexico chiles. More recently he has come up with the "Mex Big Jim" — up to 12 inches long — a bit hotter than the "6-4." It matures early and produces more chile per acre. There may be a foot long chile relleño in our future.

The nomenclature problem is further illustrated by the *chipotle*. The name comes from the *Nahuatl* words *chil* (chile) and *poctli* (smoke) and most authorities seem to agree that it's a smoked *jalapeño* chile. Our confidence in this definition was shaken by the statement in one Spanish language book that ". . . the dried *cuaresmeño* chile is called *chipotle.*" Suddenly they had taken away not only our *jalapeño* but the smoke as well. Subsequently we have found references to *chipotles* that describe them as " . . . yellow chiles in vinegar," and even a recipe calling for "fresh *chipotles.*" This is certainly a contradiction in terms or at best an honorary title conferred in anticipation of an ultimately higher use.

Actually, the chile *cuaresmeño,* or Lenten chile, was easy to dismiss as simply another name for the *jalapeño* — although there are those who insist that these are distinct chiles. In Vera Cruz the *jalapeño* has still another name. It is called the *huachinango*, presumably because it is used in cooking the fish of the same name. Or could it be named after the town of Huachinango? It seemed fitting that in the town of Huachinango we encountered two distinctly different smoked chiles being sold side by side as *chipotles.* We still think *chipotles* are smoked *jalapeños;* at least they usually are.

Quite obviously, the chile is a confusing plant, but why is it important enough for us to wade through this confusion? For one thing, more chiles are produced and consumed than any other spice in the world. With this in mind, we asked Dr. Nakayama just why he thought the chile was so popular and why it was increasing in popularity in the U.S. "Could this popularity be from some intuitively felt need for its value as a nutrition supplement?" His answer was a look that seemed to say "Unlikely." Then warming to his subject he said, "One thing about chiles — once people start eating them, they can get hooked."

Chile identification

In the above photographs of fresh and dried chiles, the names in bold type next to the chiles are the ones that will be used in the recipes in this book. Some of the other names that you are likely to encounter are listed also.

Our choice of names is necessarily arbitrary, and they will not be "correct" in many areas, so don't try to convince your grocer that he doesn't know his *pasilla* from his *ancho.*

Cooking chiles, shown above, may often be used interchangeably; in which case the recipe will call for large mild green chiles, fresh or

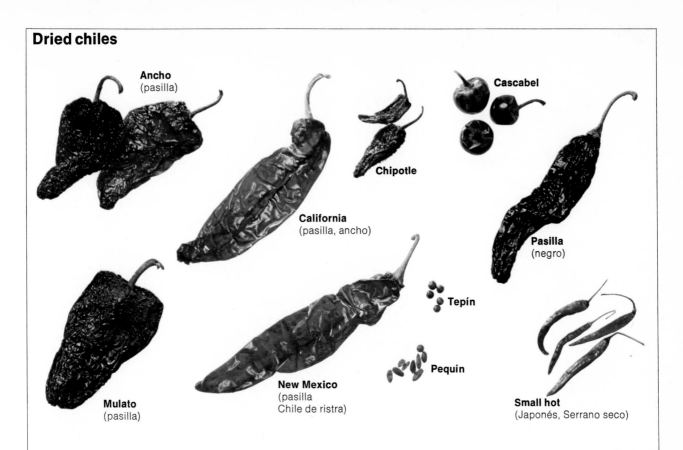

Dried chiles

Ancho (pasilla)

Chipotle

Cascabel

California (pasilla, ancho)

Pasilla (negro)

Tepín

Pequín

Mulato (pasilla)

New Mexico (pasilla Chile de ristra)

Small hot (Japonés, Serrano seco)

---

canned. If only the wide type can be used, we will specify *poblano*, which is the name most commonly used for fresh *anchos* and *mulatos* (often called *pasillas* in California.) It is important to remember that all large green chiles are not mild, so inquire and taste, if possible.

Garnish chiles usually will be specified by name in our recipes, and substitutions are generally easy in this group. There are important flavor and texture distinctions between these fresh chiles; but since they are quite hot, only the habituated and critical palate is likely to fully appreciate the distinctions. (Generally the smaller the chile the hotter, but there are enough exceptions to get you in trouble if you are incautious.)

Dried chiles are usually called by a name different from the same fresh chile. To avoid confusion we will call for *dried anchos* (or *dried pasillas*) in our recipes. (For many people this would be redundant, since to them an *ancho* means a particular broad dried chile; the fresh one they would call a *poblano*, unless, of course, they call both *pasillas*.)

Availability

The recipes in this book do not require all of the chiles shown in the photographs, since their uses often overlap. The availability of

good fresh chiles varies seasonally, even where there are good Mexican markets. The judicious use of canned, frozen and dried chiles (whole or powdered) makes preparation of most of the recipes in this book possible, most of the time, in most areas of the country.

Minimum chile supply

The chiles necessary for the recipes in this book can be obtained at most well-stocked markets. A possible exception is good powdered chile, which might be difficult to locate. *Seasoned* chile powder is widely available. The following is a basic "on-hand" list.

1. Canned mild green chiles.
2. Pickled *jalapeños en escabeche.*
3. A pure, powdered mild chile: *ancho*, California, *pasilla,* or mild New Mexico.
4. Dried chiles: *tepín, pequín, Japonés,* or other small hot chiles.

Substitutions

One of the basic substitutions you will sometimes have to make is *canned* mild green chiles instead of *fresh* mild types. Of course, you may have been foresighted enough to have a frozen supply from your garden or the market.

The other basic substitution is

the use of commercial powdered chiles as a substitute for chile pulp from dried chiles. One tablespoon of powdered chile is about equal to one dried *ancho, mulato* or *pasilla* chile.

The commonly available *seasoned* chile powder can be used if nothing else is available. It contains oregano, cumin, garlic powder and other spices. Using these powders successfully will require adjustment in the amounts of the additional spices that might also be listed in the recipe or, of course, the inclusion of seasonings you don't want.

Cayenne pepper or ground red pepper may be used as a substitute for *pequín, tepín* and the other small, hot dried chiles.

Fresh cayenne chiles, along with various other fresh chiles such as Japanese Hontakas and Louisiana hots are often available in our markets and may, in their green stage, substitute for the Mexican garnish chiles.

On occasion, we have used the grated inside pulp of bell pepper to augment the flavor of canned green chiles and to dilute the heat of some fresh green chiles. It is important, however, not to let the bell pepper flavor overpower the more subtle green chile flavor.

It is also possible to use grated bell pepper with a few drops of Tabasco when there are simply no fresh chiles available.

A word of warning

Chiles can burn the skin. Some chiles burn quickly, and some people are more sensitive than others. The potency can be deceptive because there is a delayed reaction between contact and sensation. When handling chiles, keep your hands away from your face. When finished, wash your hands thoroughly with soap and water.

The hottest part of the chile is the placental tissue that connects the seeds to the walls, so cleaning chiles exposes you more than other operations. If you are going to handle chiles for a long period, or if you have tender skin, wear rubber gloves.

Soaking green chiles in cold water with a little salt or vinegar will remove some of the heat from them. Soaking much longer than thirty minutes will begin to remove the flavor, as well as the heat.

The capsaicin, which causes the pungent or hot quality of a chile, is concentrated in the placental tissue to which the seeds are attached. The orange color of these areas in this normally mild chile indicates that this particular one may be hot, and the veins are certainly very hot.

Preparing chiles

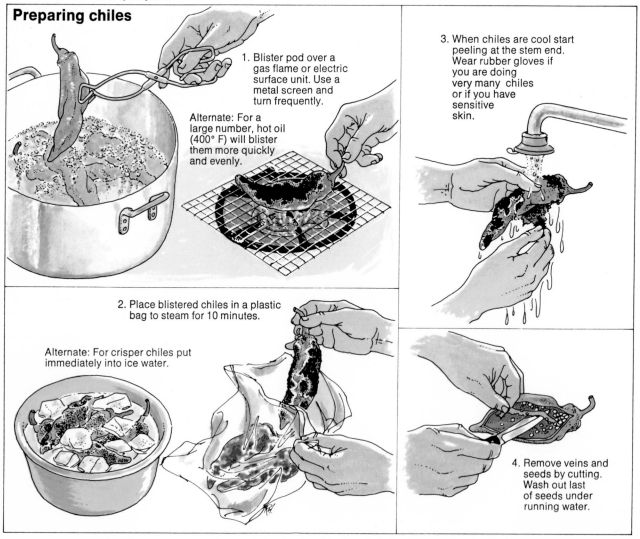

1. Blister pod over a gas flame or electric surface unit. Use a metal screen and turn frequently.

Alternate: For a large number, hot oil (400° F) will blister them more quickly and evenly.

2. Place blistered chiles in a plastic bag to steam for 10 minutes.

Alternate: For crisper chiles put immediately into ice water.

3. When chiles are cool start peeling at the stem end. Wear rubber gloves if you are doing very many chiles or if you have sensitive skin.

4. Remove veins and seeds by cutting. Wash out last of seeds under running water.

Green chiles

Green chiles are used either fresh or canned. They are used in two distinct ways:

Cooking chiles are usually roasted, peeled, seeded and deveined before use. These are the larger ones, including *poblanos, mulatos* and the mild long green California and New Mexico types. (See peeling procedure in illustration.) Chiles blistered directly over a gas flame or an electric burner will char a bit; this gives them a better flavor than those which are done with hot oil. However, when you have a large number of chiles to prepare, or want the chiles to stay especially crisp the hot oil method is valuable. It is important not to put the chiles into the oil at a rate which will reduce the temperature of the oil and cause them to cook too slowly, and thus absorb the oil. It is best to blister a few at a time, and then rinse them under cold water and peel while the oil in the pot comes back to the correct temperature. The canned large green chiles are generally peeled and seeded before canning and can be substituted for fresh ones.

Garnish chiles are used fresh or pickled *(en escabeche)*, in table *salsas* and directly as garnishes. They are not generally roasted or peeled, but the stem, seeds and membranes are sometimes removed to make them less hot. In cooked *salsas*, the chiles are simmered along with the other ingredients. *Jalapeño, serrano* and *güero* are among the most commonly used.

Whole dried chiles

Dried chiles are used in two ways: either as chile pulp or dry powder.

Chile pulp is prepared by toasting the chiles gently on a preheated *comal* or heavy frying pan, using medium heat. Toast only until chile is softened. Remove stem, membranes and seeds; open the chile and spread it flat in a sauce pan, using a small plate to weight it down. Add water to cover. Bring to a boil, reduce heat to medium, and let cook for 5 minutes. Set aside for half an hour. Place chiles in the blender briefly to mix to an even paste. For a smooth texture, strain through a sieve to remove larger skin particles.

Powdered chile. On a preheated *comal* or heavy frying pan at medium temperature, toast chiles well, turning frequently to prevent burning. Allow to cool slightly, break open and remove stem, seeds and

Colors of chile powders run from deep mahogany through brick red to brick yellow.

membrane. Crumble the chile into a *molcajete* or blender, and grind to a fine powder. (A rotary-bladed coffee mill works even better.)

Using commercial powdered chile

We have purposely used the term *powdered chile,* since most products that are simply labeled "chile powder" also contain a number of other ingredients, including cumin, oregano, onion and garlic. Pure ground chiles are available (labeled *puro*) in good Mexican markets. Chile powders from mild, medium, and hot New Mexico chiles are available (see page 96). A good powdered chile must be fresh, and should be ground without the seeds; stale powder and powder including seeds tend to be yellowish in color. The inclusion of seeds and veins is also likely to result in a hotter, but relatively less flavorful powder. Bright rich color is likely to mean fresh, good powdered chile (brick red for *anchos,* rich mahogany-red for *pasillas*).

How to preserve

Chiles can be canned, pickled, frozen and, of course, dried. The latter is the easiest way if you have an extra-big crop in your garden.

Fresh chiles, such as *jalapeños* and *serranos,* can be stored in the refrigerator in paper bags. Check these regularly for spoilage. With proper storage, they will keep about three weeks in the refrigerator. To freeze these for use in sauces, cook a few minutes, either on a dry griddle, or in a little water, before freezing.

Poblanos are roasted and peeled before freezing. They keep up to a week in the refrigerator but will gradually shrivel and lose flavor. For maximum flavor, use within three days. Roast chiles over an open flame or under the broiler until they are blistered and charred. Then, either wrap them in a damp towel and let steam for 20 minutes, or put in a plastic bag and steam 5 to 10 minutes.

If you want crisp chiles, instead of steaming them, plunge them into ice water to cool immediately after roasting. When the chiles are cool, pack in plastic bags and freeze. They can be stored in the freezer for up to a year at 0 degrees F. To use, remove as many chiles as needed, and rinse the charred skin away under running water. When thawed, remove the seeds and veins.

Chiles can be skinned, seeded, and deveined before freezing but should be frozen singly before they are packed in plastic bags — otherwise they tend to stick together. A very convenient way to have diced chiles on hand is to freeze the peeled and cleaned chiles in a thick bunch or in a rigid freezer container. Shave off as much as needed whenever chopped chiles are called for.

Under good conditions (dry and cool), dried chiles will keep well through one season's storage. For longer storage, the thoroughly dry chiles should be sealed in jars (if moisture condenses in the jar, the chiles were not dry enough). If you have room, the best place to store them is in tightly closed containers in the freezer.

The tomatillos *and garlic, as well as the* chipotle *chiles, are turned and toasted on the* comal.

Salsas

The word *salsa* literally translates as sauce, but its use in Mexico and in Mexican cook books is commonly limited to the table sauces that are used primarily as garnishes. The other sauces which are such an integral part of Mexican cooking, such as the *moles* and *pipiánes,* will be described in the appropriate chapters along with the meat or poultry they usually accompany.

A Mexican table setting is incomplete without its bowl of chile *salsa.* There are fresh *salsas,* cooked *salsas,* green ones, and red ones. The ingredients common to most are tomatoes, onions, and chiles. The "bite" may be provided by the tiny *tepín* or *pequín* chiles, or other dry ground chiles. Hot sauces can include any of a gamut of fresh chiles, such as *güeros, serranos,* or *jalapeños.*

If you have any members of your family who are in the habit of raiding the refrigerator armed with a table-spoon for sampling whatever is up front, unsealed, and even modestly tempting, give them fair warning; a tablespoon of some of these *salsas* can be incapacitating to the uninitiated.

Salsa Cruda
(Uncooked sauce)

This *salsa cruda* is a mild, subtle sauce best served chilled. We like it as a hot weather condiment with meat.

---

3 mild long green chiles, chopped
2 large tomatoes, peeled and chopped
2 small green onions or ½ small white onion, minced
1 tablespoon vinegar
1 clove garlic, minced (optional)
   Salt and pepper to taste

Mix and serve. Leftover sauce should be simmered for a few minutes and refrigerated. Makes about 2½ cups.

For a hotter sauce: Substitute *serrano* or *jalapeño* chiles, canned or fresh, seeded and chopped. Add either minced fresh cilantro or crumbled dry oregano.

Salsa Frita
(Cooked sauce)

½ small onion, minced
1 clove garlic, minced
1 tablespoon lard or shortening
2 or 3 *jalapeños,* seeds and veins removed, chopped
2 large tomatoes, peeled and chopped
   Salt and pepper
   Chopped cilantro or crumbled oregano to taste

1. Sauté onion and garlic in lard until soft.

The ingredients are combined in the molcajete *(or a blender) to make* Salsa de Chipotle.

2. Add chiles, tomatoes, salt and pepper to taste. Simmer for about 15 minutes. Add cilantro or oregano before serving. Makes about 2 cups.

Salsa Azteca
(Mexican hot sauce)

5 canned *serrano* chiles, seeded and minced or ground
5 large firm tomatoes, peeled and finely chopped
1 or 2 cloves garlic, minced or mashed
1 onion, minced
1 tablespoon fresh cilantro, chopped
1 tablespoon vinegar
1 tablespoon oil
Salt and pepper

Mix all the ingredients with the vinegar and oil. Season to taste.

This is a very hot sauce for use with meat or other dishes. It is enough for a large group. Leftover sauce will keep for at least a week to 10 days if simmered for a few minutes. Allow to cool and refrigerate. Makes about 1 quart.

Salsa Verde I
(Cooked green sauce)

A sauce which is different in taste, appearance and texture can be made by substituting *tomatillos* (Mexican green tomatoes) and using the blender.

10 or so fresh *tomatillos* or
1 can (12 oz.) *tomatillos*, drained
1 or 2 chiles, *serrano* or *jalapeño*, either fresh or canned, seeded
1 small onion, chopped
1 clove garlic
6 sprigs fresh cilantro or parsley, chopped
2 tablespoons oil
Salt and pepper to taste

If fresh *tomatillos* are used, remove dry outer husk, wash and boil in a little water until just tender. Blend all the ingredients (except the oil) in a blender for about 5 seconds. Heat the oil in a skillet and cook the mixture, stirring constantly, for 2 or 3 minutes. Serve hot or cold. This is an excellent sauce for *tacos, burritos* or as a dip. Makes about 1½ cups.

Salsa Verde II
(Uncooked green sauce)

Use *one* of the following varieties of chiles:
2 *serrano*; 1 or 2 *güero*;
1 large *jalapeño*, finely chopped
1 can (12 oz.) *tomatillos*, drained or 8 fresh *tomatillos* (½ pound)
2 cloves garlic, chopped
¼ cup cilantro, slightly chopped
½ teaspoon salt
2 green onions, finely chopped (or 3 tablespoons finely minced onion)
¼ cup water

To cook fresh *tomatillos:* Preheat *comal* or heavy frying pan over medium heat. Place the *tomatillos* on the *comal* with their husks on. Toast, turning often, until the husks are

brown and the *tomatillo* flesh is soft (about 10 minutes). Remove the husks. For alternate method of cooking *tomatillos* see *Salsa Verde I.*

To make the sauce: If using the *molcajete,* grind the ingredients in the order given, blending well between each addition. If using the blender, add all the ingredients and blend briefly to a textured purée. Makes about 1½ cups.

Salsa
(Home canned chile sauce)

1 pound onions
2 pounds fresh hot chiles
5 pounds tomatoes
2 teaspoons salt
½ teaspoon pepper
⅓ cup lemon juice or vinegar

1. Chop the onions and chiles into small pieces.

2. Peel and chop fresh tomatoes, or chop canned, whole peeled tomatoes into small pieces. Add onions, chiles and other ingredients to chopped tomatoes.

3. Pack into hot jars, seal and process in boiling water bath for 5 minutes. Alternate canning method: Bring *salsa* to a boil and pack hot into hot sterilized jars. Seal at once.

To increase or decrease hotness of the *salsa,* increase or decrease the amount of chiles in the recipe. Fresh or canned chiles may be used but fresh chiles give better flavor. Makes 6 pints.

Salsa de Chipotle
(Table chile sauce)

3 or 4 *chipotle* chiles
6 to 8 fresh *tomatillos* (½ pound)
2 cloves garlic
2 green onions, finely minced (or 3 tablespoons finely minced onion)
¼ cup water
¼ cup cilantro leaves, slightly chopped

1. Preheat the *comal* or frying pan over medium-high heat, reduce to medium-low and toast the chiles well. Set the chiles aside to cool.

2. Place the *tomatillos* (still in husks) and garlic (with skins on) onto the *comal.* Toast gently, turning often, until the husks are brown and the flesh soft, approximately 10 minutes.

3. Remove the stems from the chiles and crumble them, including the seeds, into the *molcajete* (the chiles should be crisp). Grind the chiles, peel and add the garlic cloves and grind into a paste.

4. Remove the husks and add the *tomatillos* one at a time to the mixture in the *molcajete,* blending well after each addition.

5. Add all remaining ingredients and grind to blend. Store in a glass jar in the refrigerator. Will keep 1 week. Makes 1½ cups.

Blender method: Blend the chiles into a fine powder. Add all remaining ingredients and blend briefly. Use as a table sauce to garnish *tacos, tostadas, panuchos, burritos, frijoles* and *sopas secas.*

Salsa de Jalapeños Rojos
(Fresh red *jalapeño* sauce)

3 large tomatoes (1½ pounds)
½ onion, chopped
½ teaspoon salt
2 tablespoons lard or oil
4 cloves garlic
4 fresh red *jalapeño* chiles, roasted, peeled, cleaned and cut into *rajas* (strips)
1 sprig *epazote* or 2 tablespoons cilantro leaves, slightly chopped (optional)

1. Broil the tomatoes until fork-tender and peel.

2. Place the tomatoes, chopped onion and salt into a blender and blend briefly to an even consistency.

3. Melt the lard in a skillet and add the garlic cloves. Allow the garlic to toast to a golden brown. Remove the garlic and discard.

4. Add the chile *rajas* and sauté them briefly over high heat.

5. Add the tomato purée and *epazote* and cook over high heat, stirring, until a thick textured sauce has developed, approximately 8 to 10 minutes. Serve warm over vegetables or eggs (see page 66). Makes about 3 cups.

Salsa de Chile Japonés
(A hot "garlicky" table sauce)

5 tomatillos
5 *Japonés* chiles
1 clove garlic, peeled
Salt to taste

1. Remove husks from the tomatillos. Wash the *tomatillos* and cook in a little water with the chiles for 5 minutes.

2. Remove the stems and put the chiles, *tomatillos* and garlic in the blender and blend until smooth.

3. If a thinner sauce is desired, add some of the cooking water. Salt to taste. Makes about ½ cup.

For a milder sauce, with a different flavor, vary the chiles. For example, try 1 or 2 *pasillas*, or 5 *cascabeles*. Lightly toast the chiles, remove seeds and veins. Cook the chiles for 5 minutes in a little water. Let stand for 30 minutes. Blend the chiles with a small amount of the soaking liquid. Strain if desired before blending with the *tomatillos* and garlic.

Masa dishes

The tortilla and other dishes made from this special corn dough, ground from lime treated corn kernels, were the heart of ancient cuisine. Today they remain the mainstay of contemporary Mexican cooking.

The word *masa* literally translates as dough, but in Mexico *masa* means the corn dough used for *tortillas* and other corn dishes. Dough made from wheat flour is called *masa de trigo*. In this chapter, we are including recipes for wheat flour *tortillas* as well as corn *tortillas*.

The Mexican way with corn cookery uses techniques with origins as lost in prehistory as the origins of corn itself.

Not merely the bread of Mexico, the *tortilla* is often the plate and spoon as well. This simple, unleavened disk lends itself to all manner of manipulation: It is folded over some fillings and rolled around others; it can be fried or toasted to serve as scoops, or dried and broken up to form the base for casseroles and thickening for soups.

To make *tortillas* you must have *masa*; to make *masa* you first make *nixtamal*. *Nixtamal* is quite similar to the lye hominy or *samp* that the Indians of the northeast taught the early English settlers to make. Instead of the lye leached from wood ashes, the early Mexicans used slaked lime, made by firing limestone in a kiln and quenching it with water. The process is still essentially unchanged.

For those of us who don't have time to make our own *nixtamal,* some will be lucky enough to live where freshly cooked *tortillas* can be purchased or where prepared *masa* is available. The rest of us will have to use *masa harina* which is a "flour" made from dehydrated *nixtamal;*

◁

Señora Josefa Huautla pats out blue corn masa, *for chalupas,* boat-shaped *sopes,* in the market at Acazochitlán.

it makes a good *tortilla,* but isn't quite the same as one from fresh *masa.*

Making your own *nixtamal* is a lengthy process, but if you decide to try it, be sure to use slaked lime *(calcium hydroxide),* available as "builders lime." Do *not* use unslaked lime *(calcium oxide).*

Nixtamal

5 tablespoons powdered, slaked lime
4 quarts water
2 quarts dry, white field corn

1. In an enamel or stainless steel pot, add lime to water and mix well.

2. Add corn; stirring occasionally, bring to a boil and remove from heat. Cover the pot and let corn soak for several hours (or overnight).

3. After rinsing off limewater in a colander, rub the kernels between your palms to remove the gelatinous remnants of the hulls. Don't worry about removing the dark, pointed nibs (unless you are making *tortillas* for the emperor). Rinse in at least 6 changes of water to remove all traces of lime.

4. The *nixtamal* may now be ground into *masa.* If you plan to do this on a *metate* and want *tortillas* for breakfast, you had better be up before dawn.

Today the production of *masa* and of *tortillas* has been almost completely mechanized, although hand-patted *tortillas* are still made and sold at higher prices. Even in remote villages, the grinding of the *nixtamal* into *masa* is generally done with a hand-cranked Corona type mill, rather than the *metate* and *mano;* and a *tortilla* press often replaces the thirty to forty pats that a good *tortilla* maker needs to shape each one from a ball of *masa.*

If you wonder why this complex

process is used in preference to dry grinding, just try eating a *tortilla* made out of cornmeal. The lime treatment gives a texture and flavor that can't be approached by dry grinding.

Tortillas de Maíz
(Corn *tortillas*)

2 cups *masa harina*
1¼ to 1½ cups warm water

1. Gradually work the water into the *masa harina.* Mix well and knead it hard, pushing with the heel of your hand for 3 to 5 minutes. Keep

You can watch hand-patted tortillas being made for your meal in the garden restaurant Cazadores Campestres in Tlaquepaque.

Hand-patted tortillas *require a skill that takes a long time learning.*

If it sticks to the plastic, add a little more *masa harina* to the dough. It takes a little practice to learn how the dough should feel, but it's worth it.

3. Place the *tortilla* on the hot, ungreased *comal*. Bake until the edges begin to dry, about 30 seconds. Flip and bake until lightly speckled on the underside — about 1 minute. Flip a second time and bake about 30 seconds. The side that is now up is the face of the *tortilla,* the one where the filling goes. A well-made *tortilla* will usually puff up on the second flip. The cooking time will be anywhere from 2 to 3 minutes, depending on the thickness of the *tortillas* and the temperature of the pan.

4. Wrap together in a towel or napkin as they are made, to keep them soft and warm. Makes 12.

Tortillas may be stored up to 1 week in the refrigerator. They also freeze well.

Tortillas should be served warm and must be reheated individually. The best and most traditional method is directly over a gas flame, turning constantly. If the *tortilla* is too dry and does not easily soften, dampen your hands with water and rub the *tortilla,* or steam the *tortilla* for a few seconds. They may also be reheated on a *comal* or heavy frying pan over medium-high heat. They will stay warm, wrapped together in a slightly dampened towel in a 200 degree oven.

Stale *tortillas* recycle well; for instance, use them in *Chilaquiles,* page 41, *Tortilla* Soup, page 44, and *Totopos,* page 36.

the dough wrapped in wax paper or plastic wrap while you make the *tortillas,* or the dough will dry out.

2. Put the *comal* or heavy frying pan on medium-high heat. Break off a large, walnut-size piece of dough, hand pat it 2 or 3 times to partially flatten, and place on the *tortilla* press between a folded sheet of polyethylene (about the thickness of a heavy polyethylene bag). Close the lid and press hard. Remove the *tortilla* from the press, and peel off the plastic. If you don't have a press, a rolling pin may be used.

If you have the correct amount of liquid in your dough, the plastic will peel easily off the *tortilla.* If it cracks around the edges, add a little more water and knead it in well.

To make flour tortillas: *Knead dough before starting.*

Make balls of dough by squeezing (extruding) from a fistful of dough.

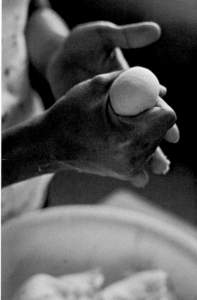

After balls are made, lightly coat each one with lard.

To make corn tortillas: *Masa is placed a bit back of center on the sheet.*

The handle exerts strong leverage to flatten the masa.

The sheet is peeled away from the finished product — a tortilla.

Tortillas de harina

Wheat flour *tortillas* are a variation of the traditional corn *tortillas,* but really common only in the north of Mexico and in the southwestern United States. In the state of Sonora, many housewives pride themselves on their paper-thin *tortillas,* which are often two feet across. Angelo Villa's mother, who was born in Moctezuma, Sonora, used to make them on special occasions. They were so thin that you could see the outlines of your fingers through them.

For ordinary use, flour *tortillas* are generally made a little larger than corn ones. A skilled *tortilla* maker can make them so perfectly round, and even in thickness, that they look as if they came out of a mold. It looks easy. But just try it!

Don't get frustrated and discouraged if your first efforts look ragged and uneven. Remember, the *tortillera* whose *tortillas* look so beautifully round, has probably been making them since she was a little girl, playing with a ball of dough while her mother prepared them for the family meal. It may seem like cheating, but there's no reason for not using the kitchen shears to trim ragged edges. And, if you're going to use them to make *burritos* or *chimichangas,* it won't matter anyway.

Here are two recipes for flour *tortillas,* one a little "shorter" (more fat) than the other.

Basic Flour Tortillas

    2 cups sifted flour
    1 teaspoon salt
    ½ teaspoon baking powder (optional)
    ¼ cup lard or shortening
    ½ cup warm water

1. Mix the sifted dry ingredients. (If you hope to make large *tortillas,* omit the baking powder, which will keep them from stretching.) Work in the lard or shortening and mix well. Now add the water and knead until the dough is springy. Divide the dough into egg-sized balls, and place them on a piece of wax paper, covered by a clean cloth, for 15 to 30 minutes.

2. Using a rolling pin, roll the dough balls into thin circles, 7 to 8 inches across, on a lightly floured board.

3. Bake on a hot, ungreased griddle until speckled with brown. Flip and cook the other side. The *tortilla* may puff up while it bakes. If so, press down lightly with a pad made of a tea towel. As they are finished, place the hot *tortillas* between the folds of a tea towel until serving time. To store them, place in a plastic bag in the refrigerator. Makes about 1 dozen large *tortillas.*

Lightly flour balls before rolling. Roll once forward and once back.

Flip and revolve ¼ turn. Repeat rolling until proper thickness is gained.

Each tortilla is baked on both sides until speckled brown and cooked through.

Wheat grown in small plots in the mountains is still threshed by hand and ground into harina de trigo *for making flour* tortillas.

Noemi's Tortillas de Harina
(Flour *tortillas*)

3 cups flour
1 tablespoon salt
½ cup lard (at room temperature)
1 to 1¼ cups hot water

1. Sift the flour and salt together. Mix in the lard with your fingers until thoroughly mixed and even textured. Add water until the dough cleans the sides of the bowl. The dough should be fairly wet. Knead well for 5 minutes, adding a little flour if necessary. Cover and let it set for at least 20 minutes.

2. When ready to make the *tortillas* give the dough a couple of kneads, then take a handful of dough, and, making a fist, squeeze out a walnut-size ball of dough between thumb and first finger. Lightly grease your hands and grease each ball of dough. When ready to roll, lightly flour the balls. Using a rolling pin, roll the *tortillas* one roll forward and one roll back, flip over and turn ¼ turn. Roll, flip and turn until the *tortilla* is very thin and round. Noemi says, "You can't roll them like pie dough. They won't come out the right shape."

3. Bake on a hot, ungreased *comal* or heavy frying pan on both sides until speckled brown and cooked through. If the *tortilla* puffs up while cooking, lightly press it down so it cooks evenly. As the *tortillas* are finished, place them between the folds of a napkin in a basket to keep warm. They may be stored in a plastic bag in the refrigerator. Makes approximately 20 *tortillas.*

Antojitos

Antojito is, literally, a "little whim." An older dictionary we have calls it a hankering, and that older American word seems to fit. *Antojitos* are generally considered snacks, but many are sufficient for the main dish of a meal. Most *antojitos* are based on *masa* cooking.

The Mexican dishes most familiar in the U.S. are the *tortilla* based *antojitos: tacos, enchiladas,* and *tostadas.* But there is another group of *masa* based *antojitos* which do not start with the *tortilla.* Of these, only *tamales* are familiar north of the border, but in Mexico there is a confusing variety of *sopes, chalupas, garnaches, tlacoyos,* and *gordas.*

In Mexico, *antojitos* are generally served as single dish snacks or even as one course in a meal, but rarely, if ever, will you find them on a "combination plate" as they are typically served in Mexican restaurants north of the border.

Tortilla Fillings
Res (Beef)

3 pounds chuck roast
3 tablespoons lard or oil
1 medium onion, diced
2 cloves garlic, crushed
1 teaspoon salt
1 teaspoon cumin
¼ teaspoon pepper
1 can (16 oz.) solid pack tomatoes, puréed in blender
Cilantro leaves to taste, slightly chopped

1. Cover meat with cold water. Bring to boil, cover, and simmer 2 to 2½ hours. Cool to handle easily. Shred meat. (Save the broth for use in soups or rice. It freezes well.)

2. Slightly brown shredded meat in lard; add onion and garlic. Allow onion to cook soft. Add salt, cumin, pepper, tomato purée and cilantro. Simmer ½ hour uncovered. Do not allow it to cook too dry. If necessary, add small amounts of beef broth or water to maintain a moist mixture.

3. Fill prepared *tortillas* and garnish individually.

For *burritos* — to increase yield, add:

1 cup precooked, peeled and diced potato, browned with meat; or

1 cup cooked pinto beans added after onion.

Filling for 12 *tacos* or 8 *burritos.*

Pollo (Chicken)

1 3-pound chicken
1 medium onion, diced
2 cloves garlic, crushed
2 tablespoons oil
1 can (12 oz.) *tomatillos,* drained and mashed
1 tablespoon white wine vinegar
½ teaspoon salt
¼ teaspoon pepper
¼ cup fresh cilantro leaves, slightly chopped (optional)
Sour cream

1. Disjoint chicken, cover with cold water. Bring to a boil, cover, and simmer 1 hour. Let cool in the broth to handle easily. Skin, bone and shred. Skim fat off broth and freeze.

2. Sauté onion and garlic in oil until soft. Add *tomatillos,* vinegar, salt and pepper. Bring to a boil, lower heat to medium and cook 5 minutes to reduce liquid.

3. Add chicken and cilantro, continue to cook uncovered approximately 10 minutes. Reduce heat to low to keep filling warm. Do not allow to cook too dry.

4. Fill prepared *tortillas* and garnish with a dab of sour cream. Makes filling for 12 *tacos* or 8 *burritos.*

Tacos

In the U.S., most people think a *taco* is a folded, fried *tortilla* filled with lettuce and anything handy. In most of Mexico, its meaning is more varied, and it takes a lot of looking to find a folded, fried *taco.* A Mexican *taco* is generally rolled and made with a soft *tortilla.* Use corn *tortillas* heated on the *comal* or griddle. The *tortilla* is rolled around a filling and garnished individually.

However, crisp *tacos* can also be good and may even border on the elegant if you become a good *taco* fryer.

Fry in ½-inch hot (425 degrees) oil. (If there is no temperature control, the oil is sufficiently hot when a small piece of *tortilla* pops immediately to the surface.) Fold *tortilla* in half with tongs, hold it in hot oil. Briefly press center of *tortilla* to bottom of the pan to flatten. Turn folded *tortilla* to the other side to cook.

For soft unfilled shells, cook briefly. For a crisp shell, cook until a deep golden brown. Drain well on paper towels and fill with either the beef or chicken filling. Suggestions for garnishes follow.

Garnishes for *tacos*: In Mexico the soft *taco* is usually garnished with no more than chile *salsa*, cilantro and minced onion. The range of possible garnishes is fun and makes for a very colorful table.

Use any or all of the following as *taco* garnishes: sour cream, guacamole or thinly sliced avocado, chile *salsa*, minced onion, chopped or thinly wedged tomato, shredded lettuce, crumbled *queso fresco* or your favorite cheese, grated.

Flautas

Flautas, meaning flutes, are like rolled *tacos* that are fried after the filling is put in. Two overlapped *tortillas* for extra strength and length are often used.

Traditional Flautas
(Rolled and fried *tacos*)

Have *one* of the following ready:
Shredded chicken mixture (page 32) with ¼ teaspoon oregano added
Shredded beef mixture (page 32) with ¼ teaspoon oregano added
Frijoles refritos (page 78)
2 dozen corn *tortillas*
1 recipe *guacamole sauce* (page 76)
1 recipe *chipotle sauce* (page 27) or your favorite table sauce

1. Preheat the *comal* or griddle over medium high heat. Preheat ½-inch oil in frying pan, 400 to 425 degrees.

2. Heat the *tortilla* only to soften. Fill with approximately 2 teaspoons of the prepared meat or bean mixture. Roll tightly and secure at both ends with toothpicks.

3. Lightly salt and fry in oil until golden, but not too crisp. Drain on paper toweling. Remove toothpicks.

4. On a large serving platter or individual plates, place 2 or 3 *flautas* per serving on a small bed of shredded lettuce. Top with *guacamole* sauce and serve with *chipotle* sauce.

Flautas may be made in advance and reheated in a 350 degree oven for 10 to 15 minutes. They freeze well. Makes 24 *flautas*.

Additional fillings
In addition to the beef and chicken fillings, other typical recipes for filling *burritos, flautas, sopes* and *tacos* are:

Carnitas, page 58
'Machaca, page 51
Chorizo and Egg, page 66
Chorizo and Potato, page 61
Eggs with *Nopales*, page 67
Eggs with Squash Blossoms, page 67
Eggs with Brains, page 67
Chile Verde, page 57 or any other leftover stew
Ropa Vieja, page 55

Burritos and chimichangas

Burritos and *chimichangas* are tubular "sandwiches" made of flour *tortillas*. The only difference between them is that *chimichangas* are deep fried.

1. The *tortillas* are wrapped around a filling made of shredded beef or chicken, refried beans, sometimes rice as well, and cheese. The top and bottom are folded in before being rolled. They can be held together with a toothpick.

Fry the *chimichangas* for a minute or two in an inch of hot lard or oil. Drain on paper towels.

Burritos and *chimichangas* are served warm with any of the following garnishes: chile *salsa*, avocado slices, raw onion, radish slices, sour cream, and grated cheese. They are great for using up leftovers. For suggested fillings, see page 32.

These *flautas (flutes)* are filled with shredded chicken, rolled, fried and then garnished with guacamole and crumbled cheese.

Enchiladas

Enchiladas are "chilied" tortillas. Behind that simple definition there is probably the greatest variety of dishes that come under one name in Mexican cooking. You can put a lot of different things in a *taco,* but with *enchiladas* you can vary the filling, the sauce, the topping and the garnish. The *tortillas* can then be rolled, folded or stacked. That's a lot of possible combinations. In northern Mexico and the American southwest, *enchiladas* made with a red chile sauce are most common. From Mexico City south, the distinctive *mole* sauce is more common.

Like so many other seemingly complicated dishes, *enchiladas* are quite easy if you're organized. If the ingredients are properly laid out, it takes little more time to make sixty than it does for a dozen. With student helpers to open packs of *tortillas,* and to carry the baking dishes in and out, we have put together 104 *enchiladas* for a college party in an hour or so.

For speed and efficiency, set up a production line. Have handy a stack of 12 soft *tortillas,* a skillet with hot oil, prepared heated chile sauce, a large empty plate on which to fill and roll the *enchiladas,* bowls of cheese, meat, onions, olives, and other ingredients, and finally, the baking dish into which the rolled *enchiladas* are placed for baking.

Enchiladas Sonorenses
(*Enchiladas* Sonora)

Prepare *enchiladas* as for *Enchiladas Coloradas,* but, instead of rolling after frying, stack like pancakes. Sprinkle cheese and onion mixture between each layer and on top. A variation is to top each stack with a fried egg and another spoonful of sauce.

Enchiladas de Mole

    1 dozen corn *tortillas*
    Oil for frying, ¼ inch deep
    1 jar (8 oz.) prepared *mole poblano*
      paste
    3½ cups chicken broth

For the sauce, pour the oil that has separated from the contents of the jar into a skillet. Heat the oil, add the *mole* paste and briefly fry (2-3 minutes) over medium heat. Slowly add the chicken broth, stirring constantly. Bring to a boil, then reduce to simmer. Keep warm for *tortilla* preparation. Fill with one of the fillings below.

◁

Enchiladas may be stacked or rolled or folded, as long as they are "chilied" — the variations in fillings, sauces and garnishes offer endless possibilities.

Chicken filling

    1 3-pound chicken
    2 tablespoons oil
    1 onion, chopped
    2 cloves garlic, crushed
    1 teaspoon salt
    ¾ cup *mole* sauce
    ½ cup sour cream
    ¼ cup cilantro leaves, slightly chopped
    ½ pound Monterey jack cheese
      (¼ pound grated, ¼ pound sliced)

1. Disjoint chicken, cover with cold water. Bring to a boil, cover and simmer 1½ hours. Cool to handle easily. Skin, bone and chunk. (Remove fat from broth and save broth.)

2. In skillet heat oil, sauté onion and garlic until transparent. Add chicken pieces, salt and *mole.* Reduce heat to simmer. Add sour cream and cilantro.

3. Lightly fry *tortillas* in ¼ inch hot oil, dip into warm *mole* sauce. Fill *tortilla* with slices of cheese and approximately 2 tablespoons chicken filling.

4. Roll and place in ovenproof pan. Sprinkle with grated cheese, tightly cover pan with foil; bake at 350 degrees for 15 minutes. Makes 12.

Cheese filling

    1 pound mild cheddar
    1 can (4 or 5 oz.) sliced olives
    1 onion, diced

1. Grate ¼ pound of the cheese, slice remainder. Drain olives and combine with the onion.

2. Fry *tortillas* lightly in ¼ inch hot oil, dip into warm *mole* sauce. Fill prepared *tortilla* with slices of cheese and approximately 1 tablespoon onion and olive mixture.

3. Roll and place seam side down in an ovenproof pan. Top with grated cheese. Tightly cover pan with foil and bake 15 minutes in 350 degree oven. Garnish with dab of sour cream or *guacamole,* cilantro leaves, black olives and a sprinkle of toasted sesame seeds. Makes 12.

Enchiladas Rancheras
(Ranch style *enchiladas*)

An elegant and interesting variation from the usual *enchiladas* is this tasty combination of green chile sauce and a chicken and cheese filling. We use the fresh Anaheim or canned green chiles, although one of the hotter varieties would more commonly be used in Mexico. If you know that your guests prefer chile with more "bite," add a couple of seeded and chopped *jalapeño* chiles to your sauce. Or, a good green *salsa* made with *serrano* or *jalapeño* chiles can be served to those who prefer a hotter taste.

    2 cans (7 oz. each) mild green chiles,
      chopped, or 5 to 7 fresh Anaheim
      chiles, roasted, peeled, cleaned and
      chopped
    2 cans (12 oz. each) *tomatillos*
      (Mexican green tomatoes)
    1 small onion chopped
    3 cups water, or chicken broth
    2 cloves garlic, minced
    2 teaspoons salt
    1 bay leaf
    4 tablespoons cornstarch
    1 dozen corn *tortillas*
      Oil for frying
    ½ pound jack cheese, grated
    ½ pound longhorn or mild cheddar,
      grated
    2 cups shredded or diced cooked
      chicken or cooked lean pork
    1 pint sour cream
    2 avocados, peeled and cut into strips

1. Blend the first six ingredients in an electric blender. Put the mixture in a skillet, add the bay leaf, cover and simmer 30 minutes. Remove bay leaf. Mix cornstarch in ¼ cup water and combine with the chile mixture. Cover and set aside.

2. Fry the *tortillas* in hot oil only long enough to soften. Do not allow them to get too crisp to roll.

3. Dip the fried *tortillas* in the green chile mixture. Fill each with some of the combined grated jack and cheddar cheese and some chicken or pork. Roll and arrange in a baking dish. Top with the remaining green chile sauce.

4. Bake at 350 degrees just long enough to heat through, about 15 minutes. Serve at once with sour cream and garnish with avocado slices. Makes 12.

For a company dish, mash the avocados for a *guacamole,* salt to taste, then use a cake decorator to top the *enchiladas* with ornamental ribbons of avocado and dabs of sour cream. Garnish with shredded lettuce and radish slices.

Enchiladas Coloradas
(Red chile *enchiladas*)

    1 can (10 oz.) red chile sauce
    1 can (6 oz.) tomato sauce
    ½ pound jack cheese
    ½ pound longhorn or mild cheddar
    1 can (6 to 8 oz.) pitted medium-size
      ripe olives
    ½ teaspoon dry oregano leaves,
      crushed
      Salt
      Lard or oil for frying
    2 green onions with tops, chopped

1. Heat the chile and tomato sauces together. Salt to taste.

2. Grate the two cheeses. Toss them to mix together but do not pack.

3. Halve 12 olives and set aside as a decorative topping. Chop the rest of the olives and mix with the onion and the oregano.

The tortilla *is picked up with tongs and transferred to the grease with its "face" (least speckled) side up.*

With a natural lift-and-swing motion, the tortilla *is transferred to the chile sauce, so that the face side is now down.*

The chilied tortilla *now lands, using the same swinging transfer with the face side up for the filling step.*

4. Fry each *tortilla* on one side only, but not enough to make it stiff.
Dip the fried *tortilla* in the hot sauce. Remove and fill the uncooked side with a tablespoon of the chopped onion and olive, and some of the grated cheese. Roll and lay seam side down in a baking dish.

5. When all the *tortillas* are stuffed and rolled, spoon the remaining sauce over them, especially the open ends. Sprinkle the rest of the cheese over the top. Decorate each *enchilada* with two olive halves.

6. Bake at 350 degrees for 10 minutes, or until the cheese is melted. Sprinkle green onion over the top and serve. Makes 12 *enchiladas.*

Salsa de Chile Colorado
(Red cooking sauce for
beef or cheese *enchiladas)*
This red *enchilada* sauce is made in the traditional manner.

```
3 dried ancho chiles
3 dried Anaheim chiles
2 pasilla chiles
3 cups water
2 cloves garlic, minced
1 teaspoon salt
½ teaspoon oregano
¼ teaspoon cumin
⅛ scant teaspoon powdered cloves
3 tablespoons lard or oil
2 tablespoons flour
3½ cups liquid (liquid from the chiles
    and chicken broth to make 3½
    cups total)
```

1. Warm the chiles on the *comal* or griddle to soften. Remove and discard the stems and seeds.

2. Place the chiles in a saucepan and cover with the water. Weight the chiles down with a small plate. Bring to a boil, reduce heat to medium and cook for 5 minutes. Set aside for 30 minutes.

3. Drain the chiles and reserve the liquid. Discard any tough pieces of skin, after scraping the pulp from it.

4. Place the chiles in the blender, together with the garlic, salt, oregano, cumin and cloves. Blend to a smooth purée. Strain for a smooth-textured sauce.

5. In a skillet, heat the lard and lightly toast the flour. Add the chile purée and fry for 3 minutes, stirring constantly. Measure the chile liquid and add sufficient chicken broth to measure 3½ cups. Slowly stir in the liquid. Bring to a boil, reduce heat to simmer and cook 5 minutes. Makes about 3½ cups.

Enchiladas de Carne
(Meat *enchiladas)*

Prepare ingredients as for *Enchiladas Coloradas* but use the shredded beef filling, page 32. Reduce cheese to ¼ pound, and sprinkle over the top of the *enchiladas* before baking.

Enchiladas Suizas
("Swiss" *enchiladas)*

Follow the recipe for *Enchiladas Rancheras* but do not top with the sour cream and avocado. After adding the green chile sauce to the rolled *enchiladas,* cover evenly with one cup of heavy cream. Then bake, uncovered, in a preheated oven at 350 degrees for about 15 minutes. Serve hot. Makes 12 enchiladas.

Tostadas

Tostadas are corn *tortillas* fried flat and crisp and topped with fried beans, shredded meat, lettuce and cheese — a whole meal on an edible plate.

1. Use corn *tortillas.* Lightly salt *tortillas* on each side. Heat ¼-inch deep oil to 425 degrees. Fry flat on both sides until a crisp, deep golden brown. Drain on paper towels.

2. Spread with *frijoles refritos.*
3. Top with shredded meat or chicken.

4. Garnish with sour cream, thinly sliced avocado, *chile salsa,* chopped tomatoes, shredded lettuce. Top with radish slices, whole ripe olives, crumbled *queso fresco,* or your favorite cheese, grated.

Totopos or tostaditas

Totopos or *tostaditas* are triangular pieces of crisp-fried *tortilla,* usually used for scooping up dips. They are sometimes served with refried beans, green chile, and melted cheese. With just the cheese and chile, they are called *nachos.*

Use corn *tortillas.* Cut in quarters sixths, or eighths, as desired. Lightly salt. Fry as for *tostadas.*

Tostadas and *totopos* may be prepared ahead and reheated in a 350 degree oven.

Quesadillas

In the southwest, *quesadillas* are *tortillas* folded over a filling of chile and cheese. In Mexico they are more varied in fillings and are made by folding an uncooked corn *tortilla* over a filling, pinching the edges together, and frying. Precooked *tortillas* are often used. In the southwestern U.S., flour *tortillas* are preferred.

In their simplest form, *quesadillas* are the Mexican equivalent of a toasted cheese sandwich, but in the form of a *taco.* Put grated cheese

After filling and rolling, coat the enchiladas (paying particular attention to covering the ends) with extra chile sauce.

on one half of a corn *tortilla,* fold and pin together with toothpicks. Fry in oil or butter until almost crisp and drain on absorbent paper or toast them on a ungreased *comal.* We find that they taste better with a little salt.

Quesadillas con Nopales
(*Quesadillas* with cactus)

Corn *tortillas* (flour *tortillas* may be used)
Fresh whole *nopales* (cactus sections)
**Queso Panela, Monterey jack or mild
   cheddar (2 slices per serving)**
**Sour cream, *chile salsa, chile rajas*
   (strips)**

1. Preheat the *comal* over medium heat.

2. Clean, trim, wash and slice each *nopal* in half, lengthwise.

3. Slightly dampen the *tortilla* and place on the *comal.* Turn and place the *nopal* slice and cheese on one half of the *tortilla.*

4. Fold the *tortilla* in half and gently toast on both sides until the *nopal* is tender and the cheese melted. If desired, open the *tortilla* and add a dab of sour cream and chile.

Traditional Quesadillas

The most traditional *quesadilla* is a turnover made of *masa,* rather than a precooked *tortilla,* with a filling that usually includes cheese and may include meats, beans, or *tamál* fillings.

---

   2 cups *masa harina*
   2 tablespoons flour
   ½ teaspoon baking powder
   2 tablespoons melted butter
   1 egg, lightly beaten
   ½ teaspoon salt
   ½ cup milk

1. Mix the dry ingredients. Add the other ingredients, the milk last, using only enough of the milk to make the dough fairly stiff.

2. Using a *tortilla* press, form small *tortillas* 3 or 4 inches across. Add filling of your choice. Fold over and seal edge.

3. Fry in hot lard or oil (400 degrees). Drain on absorbent paper and serve hot. Makes approximately 1 dozen. Suggested fillings:

   Frijoles Refritos (page 78)

   Cheese with strips of green chiles (or hotter varieties, if desired)

   Meat or fowl and cheese in *Adobo, Mole* or *Pipián* (pages 54 and 65)

   Meat or chicken *Picadillo* (page 61)

Another type of *quesadilla* is deep-fried dough balls or sticks. Use the *masa* recipe above, add grated Romano or Parmesan cheese. Mix well. Form into small balls or rolls. Deep fry and serve hot.

Garnish Enchiladas Coloradas with shredded longhorn and Monterey jack cheese, chopped onions and sliced olives. Reheat the whole dish in the oven just long enough for the cheese to start melting.

Tortillas Rellenas
(Stuffed *tortillas*)

1 pound cooked, shredded pork
1 tablespoon lard
1 onion, chopped
1 large tomato, finely chopped
  Salt and pepper to taste
3 eggs, separated
1 dozen *tortillas*
  Flour
  Oil for frying
  Salsa (page 39)
  Avocado, onion slices, sprig of cilantro
  for garnish

1. Sauté the pork in the lard until brown, add onion, cook until soft. Add tomatoes, season with salt and pepper and cook until thickened.

2. Beat egg whites until stiff, fold in yolks and mix until blended.

3. Place some of the meat mixture on a *tortilla,* roll and secure with a toothpick.

4. Lightly dust the rolled *tortilla* with flour and dip in the egg batter.

5. Fry in medium-hot oil until the batter is set.

6. Serve with *salsa* and garnish.

with avocado and onion slices and a sprig of cilantro. Makes 12.

Variation: We find this recipe very good substituting ½ pound meat and 1 cup of cooked, diced potato for the 1 pound of meat.

Thick masa dishes

Sopes, tamales and other favorite Mexican dishes can be designated as thick *masa* creations. That is to say, they don't start out as thin *tortillas* but are made from fresh *masa*.

Gordas are little fat *tortillas*, sometimes made with thick cream or mashed potatoes added to the *masa*. When a *gorda* is made in a shape like a flat football it becomes a *memelo*, if this has a filling it becomes a *clacollo* (or *tlacoyo*). If this elongated shape has raised edges to hold meat, *salsa* or other things it is called a *chalupa* after the canoe-shaped boat of that name. If the same raised edge construction is made circular it's probably a *sope* or *sopita*. Most of

these are fried but some are cooked on the dry *comal,* and some are cooked first on the dry *comal* and then fried.

Enedina's Sopes

¼ teaspoon baking soda
¼ teaspoon salt
¼ cup chicken broth or water
1 pound *masa* (from the *tortillería,* or
  made from *masa harina*)
2 to 3 tablespoons lard
  Oil for frying

1. Dissolve baking soda and salt in chicken broth. Pour over the *masa*. Soften the lard by rubbing between your hands. Mix all together and knead until well mixed and light. Dough should be fairly moist, but still workable.

2. Moisten your hands with water; form *masa* into walnut-size balls, and pat to approximately 3-inch size *tortillas*, ¼ inch thick. Bake on a medium-hot *comal* or frying pan on both sides to partially set the *masa*. Pinch up the edge about ⅝ inch to form a container for the filling.

Pat masa *into cakes about 3 inches across and ¼ inch thick.*

Partially cook the cakes on a dry comal *to set* masa.

Pinch up edges of partially baked masa *to form rim of* sope.

Fry sopes, *then spoon hot fat into centers to cook top surface.*

3. Fry the *sopes* one at a time in ¼ inch hot oil or lard (400 degrees) until golden brown. Spoon the hot grease into the center of the *sope* to cook it. Drain on paper towels.

Filling

- **1 dried *ancho* chile**
- **½ pound ground pork**
- **1 small potato**
- **1 clove garlic, chopped**
- **1 tomato, chopped**
- **1 small onion, chopped**
- **2 *serrano* chiles, deveined, seeded and diced**
- **Pinch of cumin**
- **Queso añejo, cheddar or Monterey jack cheese**
- **Shredded lettuce or cabbage**

1. Remove the seeds and veins from the *ancho* chile. Wash. Soak in ½ cup boiling water for 30 minutes.

2. Form the ground pork into a ball. Put in boiling water and cook for 30 minutes. Remove and drain. Cook the potato in the meat water. Drain, peel and dice.

3. Put the garlic, tomato, onion, soaked chile, and the soaking water into the blender and blend until smooth.

4. Crumble the pork into small pieces, fry in 1 tablespoon hot lard for 5 minutes. Lower the heat and add the blended sauce; cook, stirring until thick. Add the diced chiles and a dash of cumin. Add diced potato, and mix well.

Salsa

- **2 large tomatoes**
- **1 *serrano* chile**
- **½ teaspoon salt**
- **Water**
- **Onion rings**
- **Cilantro**

1. Cook the tomatoes, chile, and salt in boiling water until soft. Remove from water and skin the tomatoes.

2. Place the tomatoes and the chile (stem removed) in the blender and blend until smooth. Add additional salt if necessary.

3. Place in a bowl, top with onion rings and a little cilantro.

To Assemble:

1. Sprinkle a little finely grated cheese on the cooked *sopes*.

2. Add a spoonful of meat mixture.

3. Top with finely chopped lettuce or cabbage, and more grated cheese.

4. Serve with *salsa*. May be reheated in a low oven. Serves 6 to 8.

Sopitos de Colima
Little *sopes*

- ***Masa* for *sopito* shells**
- **Meat filling (recipe below)**
- **Parmesan or Romano cheese**
- **Sliced onions, shredded lettuce, radishes for garnish**

1. Form small olive-size balls of *masa*. Press them out, either by hand or in a *tortilla* press, into two-inch circles.

2. Cook on a very lightly greased griddle or *comal*. When firm enough to handle, remove from the griddle, allow to cool slightly. Form a lip or raised edge around each and lay aside to be fried later.

Meat filling

- **1 pound lean ground beef**
- **1 or 2 cloves garlic, minced**
- **1 teaspoon salt**
- **Pinch of ground cumin (about ⅛ teaspoon)**
- **1 large tomato, chopped**
- **5 or 6 *tomatillos*, husked, or 1 additional tomato**
- **1 or 2 *jalapeño* chiles, chopped**
- **1 cup water**

1. Simmer all the ingredients together for 30 minutes.

2. Deep fry *sopito* shells until crisp in hot oil (400 degrees). Drain on paper towels.

3. Put a spoonful of the meat mixture into each shell. Top with grated Parmesan or Romano cheese and garnish with sliced onion, shredded lettuce and radishes. Serve at once. Serves 4 to 6.

Tamales

Tamales (the singular is *tamál*, although called *tamale* in English) are made throughout Mexico. They are generally *masa* spread on corn husks, and wrapped around a variety of fillings. Most Americans, even in the southwest where Mexican foods head the popularity list, are familiar only with the "hot tamale" of the restaurant combination plate or the frozen foods section of their local market. But this chile-and-meat-stuffed *tamál* is but one of an infinite variety, different in size, form and ingredients. There are *tamales* of

Serve sopes *with a pork and chile filling and a shredded cabbage and cheese garnish.*

There are many ways to wrap a tamale, but the wrapping must always hold the masa *in and keep the steam out.*

pork, beef, cracklings, venison and other game, poultry, seafood, beans, beans and chile, fresh corn and chile, and many more.

Then there are the sweet or breakfast *tamalitos,* small ones with fillings of all kinds of fruits and nuts, sweet and spiced beans, and even caramel.

There are even *tamales* with no filling other than *masa,* which substitute as a kind of bread. In the tropical Gulf Coast, and around Oaxaca, *tamales* are wrapped, not in corn husks, but in banana leaves, which impart a very distinctive flavor.

The sweet *tamalitos* are really too heavy to be a dessert but are delicious as snacks or for breakfast. These have fillings of fruits, nuts, raisins and beans, sweetened and spiced with cinnamon and cloves, sweetened fresh corn, and even candied fruits and caramel.

Tamales are party and festival fare — for any time that families and friends get together: birthdays, chistenings, weddings, All Saint's Day, New Year's. The old saying about "Too many cooks . . ." doesn't apply to a *tamalada,* a *tamales* making get-together. There are plenty of jobs to go around at any age level.

The first task is to soak and clean the *hojas* (corn leaves), laying aside any which are torn or worm-holed (only fit for tearing into strings to tie the ends of the filled *tamales*) and to separate the good ones by size, standing them up to drain until they are needed. Later, you must tie the ends of the completed *tamales.* Finally, you must mix the great pans of lard and *masa* until their smoothness and lightness are satisfactory.

We are sure that modern canning kettles will work just as well, but to this day we use an empty

ten-pound lard can with a tight-fitting lid as our *tamales* steamer. To separate the boiling water from the *tamales,* we place tomato sauce cans with the ends cut out in the bottom of the can, and on top of them a bed of corn husks. After each *tamalada,* the can is carefully washed, dried, and stored away until the next fiesta.

Traditional Tamales

- **1 pound *hojas* (dried corn husks)**
- **4 pounds pork butt or other pork roast (which should not be fatty, but have some fat for texture and flavor)**
- **2 cloves garlic**
- **1 pound dried *ancho* chiles or canned red chile *salsa***
- **Flour for thickening sauce**
- **½ teaspoon crushed dried oregano**
- **1 pound lard or other solid shortening**
- **4 pounds *masa***
- **Salt to taste**

1. Soak the husks in hot water and remove any corn silk or other matter. Stand clean husks to drain until

needed but do not allow to dry out again before use.

2. Cover the meat with water and simmer until almost tender, along with the cloves of garlic. Remove the garlic and discard when the meat is ready. Cube the meat into ½ inch pieces or smaller, and add to the chile sauce when it is done. Reserve the broth for later use in making the chile sauce.

3. Rinse dried chiles in cold water to clean. Remove stems and seeds. Reserve some seeds if a hotter sauce is desired. Open the chiles and place flat in a saucepan using a small plate to weight them down. Add water to cover and boil for 5 minutes. Remove from heat and allow to cool. Drain the chiles and discard the liquid. Place the chiles in a blender, a few at a time, using some of the broth from the meat. Blend. Strain through a sieve to remove bits of chile skin. If a hotter sauce is desired, grind the reserved seeds and add them to the finished sauce. Toast a little flour in a small amount of oil, but do not allow to burn. Add the chile sauce to the toasted flour. Season with the oregano and salt to taste. Add cooked pork.

4. In a very large bowl, beat the lard, adding cold water until it will absorb no more of it. The lard should be quite fluffy. Add the *masa* to the lard and mix thoroughly, using the ball of the hand to break down any lumps. Add some of the meat broth to achieve desired consistency, that is, dry enough to hold together and moist enough to spread easily. A small ball of the dough should rise in a glass of cold water when tested. Salt to taste.

5. Holding the broadest husks in the palm of the hand, spread a thin layer of *masa* in the form of a square in the center of each husk. The back of a tablespoon is an effective spreader. Put a large spoonful of the meat and chile mixture in the middle of the *masa* square. Roll the husk over the meat, being careful not to squeeze. Wrap with a second husk that has also been spread with a thin layer of *masa.* Tie at both ends with strips of husk or pieces of string. (Ideally, two or three persons working together should perform this operation.) Clip off excess husk with kitchen shears. The whole spreading, filling, and tying operation is much easier if the meat mixture is cold.

6. Make a layer of corn husks in a steamer and carefully stand the finished *tamales* on one end. Steam

for one hour. Allow the *tamales* to drain a few minutes before serving.

Each pound of *masa* will make about 12 good-sized *tamales.*

Tamales Blancos
(Unfilled *tamales*)

1 package corn husks
½ cup lard
2 cups *masa harina*
1 teaspoon salt
1½ teaspoons baking powder
1½ cups warmed chicken broth

1. Soak the corn husks in hot water to soften.

2. Beat the lard until fluffy.

3. Stir the dry ingredients together. Gradually beat the *masa* mixture and broth into the lard, alternately. Beat well (approximately 5 minutes). When done, a small ball of the dough should rise in a glass of cold water.

4. Place 6 to 8 cups water and a coin (see below) into the bottom of the steamer. Shake excess water from the corn husks. Line the steamer well with corn husks.

5. Spread approximately 2 tablespoons of dough on the center of each husk, roll firmly and turn bottom of the husk up. If necessary, roll in an additional husk, and/or tie with a piece of string to secure.

6. Pack *tamales* upright into steamer as they are made. Surround with corn husks. Top with terry toweling and secure lid. Bring to a boil over high heat. Reduce to medium and steam for 1½ to 2 hours. Listen for the clicking sound of the coin. It will let you "hear" the water level. When the coin becomes silent, the water level is too low and you must add more water. The *tamál* is done when it falls cleanly away from the husk.

To reheat, place the *tamál* on an ungreased *comal* over medium low and heat through, turning occasionally, until the husks are browned. If preferred, the *tamales* may be wrapped in foil and reheated in a 350 degree oven 20 to 30 minutes. *Tamales* also freeze well. Makes 12 small *tamales.*

Chilaquiles con Salsa
(Tortilla wedges simmered in a chile sauce)

1 dozen corn *tortillas* (if not stale, dry slowly in 200 degree oven)
¼ inch lard, melted for frying
1 tablespoon lard (if using homemade *chorizo*)
½ to 1 pound *chorizo* (1 to 2 cups homemade)
½ onion chopped
2 large tomatoes, chopped
1½ cups chicken broth
⅓ cup cilantro leaves
 Garnish: crumbled *queso fresco,* sour cream, finely chopped onion, avocado wedges.

1. Cut the *tortillas* into wedges, lightly salt and fry in hot lard until "chewy" and tough — not crisp. Drain on paper toweling.

2. In a large pot, melt the 1 tablespoon of lard, add the *chorizo* and cook 15 minutes over medium low heat. Add the onion and tomatoes and cook until soft. Add the broth; bring to a boil.

3. Add the prepared *tortilla* wedges and reduce heat to simmer. Cook 5 to 8 minutes, scraping the bottom often.

4. Stir in the cilantro. Garnish and serve. Serves 4.

Typical additions: 2 eggs per serving — lightly whipped and added the last few minutes, to set; or cheese slices, added the last few minutes, to melt.

Chilaquiles de Oaxaca
(Oaxaca style *tortilla* casserole)

We are indebted for this recipe to Mrs. Ida Jaqua of the Valley College Department of Family and Consumer Studies. The distinctive feature of this dish is the special flavor derived from the toasted avocado leaves. (See Ingredients, page 14.) Unfortunately, though avocados can be purchased in large markets throughout the country, securing the leaves is another problem. Luckily, the plant can be grown indoors easily. (See page 19.)

4 cups black beans (either freshly cooked or canned)
1 or 2 small *chipotle* chiles
2 cloves garlic, in thin slices
¼ inch lard or oil for frying
12 day-old *tortillas*
1 pound jack cheese, grated
6 avocado leaves

1. Blend beans and chiles. If there is not enough juice from cooked beans, add water to make 4 cups of wet purée.

2. Sauté garlic in fat; remove garlic.

3. Roll *tortillas,* slice crosswise in ½ inch slices, and fry in hot fat until light brown; drain.

4. Place half the *tortilla* slices in a shallow casserole. Cover with half the grated cheese and half the bean purée. Repeat with the second half of *tortilla,* cheese and purée.

5. Toast avocado leaves under broiler until light brown. Lay on top of bean mixture.

6. Cover and bake at 350 degrees for 30 minutes.

7. Remove leaves before serving. Serves 6.

Soups and dry soups

The soup that starts the main meal of the day is a light soup. But the soup kitchen of Mexico includes many hearty soups with two or even more meats and enough vegetable garnishes to serve as the soup main dish and salad courses.

Soups are taken very seriously in Mexico: a dinner without soup is only a snack. Soups may be *caldos* or *sopas:* The first is a clear broth with or without other solid ingredients, the latter a heavier soup.

The "dry" soup, *sopa seca,* is quite another matter. It is a soup in name only, a soupless soup. *Sopa seca* is usually rice with onions, tomatoes, and garlic cooked in a broth which is entirely absorbed or cooked away. It is also made with vermicelli or with dry *tortilla* pieces as a base.

The origin of the dry "soup" usage seems to be lost; but, if we think of it as a *dried* soup, it doesn't seem too mysterious. A *sopa seca* is, after all, at least as soupy as a martini is dry.

Crema de Aguacate
(Cream of avocado soup)

2 large ripe avocados, seeded and peeled
½ teaspoon salt
1 cup half-and-half
2 teaspoons lemon juice
2 cups chicken broth
¼ cup dry sherry

1. Place avocados, salt, cream, and lemon juice into blender. Blend to a smooth purée.

2. Heat chicken broth,. Pour purée into warmed bowls or tureen, slowly add hot broth. Add sherry.

3. Garnish with a thin slice of lime, avocado or sprig of cilantro or dab of sour cream.

4. Serve warm or chilled. To reheat, use a double boiler. Serves 6.

◁

Señora Anastacia Refas de López serves a rich potato soup in El Mercado Libertad.

Sopa de Chile Verde
(Green chile soup)

3 bell peppers
4 mild, long green chiles, roasted, peeled, and cleaned or, if available, 6 *poblano* chiles roasted, peeled, and cleaned
1 small onion, chopped
½ cup cream
1 quart consommé or beef stock
2 tablespoons butter or margarine
2 tablespoons flour
Salt and pepper
6 ounces cream cheese

1. Wash the bell peppers, snip off stems and discard; simmer in water in covered pan for 5 minutes. Drain, peel, cut open, discard seeds and veins, and cut into strips.

2. Combine the bell pepper, chiles, onion, and cream, and blend until smooth, using some of the consommé if more liquid is needed to blend.

3. Melt the butter. Blend in the flour. Stirring constantly, gradually add the bell pepper, chile mixture, and the rest of the consommé. Add salt and pepper to taste.

4. Stir until soup is thickened and smooth. Remove from the stove and serve hot with generous dabs of the cream cheese. Serves 6.

Sopa de Flor de Calabaza
(Squash or pumpkin blossom soup)

1 pound squash or pumpkin blossoms
2 tablespoons butter
½ small onion, chopped
4 cups chicken broth
Sprig of *epazote*
Salt and pepper to taste
Cream version: 1 cup half-and-half

1. Wash and chop the blossoms. In a soup pot melt the butter and gently saute the blossoms and onion.

2. Add the chicken broth and *epazote.* Simmer 20 minutes.

3. Remove the *epazote.* Add salt and pepper to taste and serve.

For cream version: Follow the above method adding the half-and-half just before serving and allowing to heat through. Serves 6.

Sopa de Melón Escribe
(Cantaloupe soup)

½ cup half-and-half
1 cup cooked, peeled and diced potato
3 cups peeled and diced cantaloupe
¼ cup dry sherry
Pinch of salt

1. Place the half-and-half, potato, and cantaloupe in the blender. Blend to a smooth purée.

2. Stir in sherry. Season to taste. Serve chilled. If desired, garnish with a sprinkle of nutmeg or lime slice. Serves 6.

Squash blossoms were used by the Aztecs and are still used for soups and in fillings for tacos and quesadillas.

The chicken pieces for Caldo de Pollo are cut to order for Señorita Enedina Gómez.

Getting to market early gets today's best vegetables for today's soup.

The vegetables are cut for eye appeal as much as eating convenience.

Pozole de Lujo, Estilo Jalisco

(Hog and hominy soup,
deluxe Jalisco style)

There are many versions of *pozole*. Most start with corn, the type called *cacahuazincle,* which is first made into hominy. Some versions add beans or even substitute garbanzos for the hominy. (In Spain *pozole* means boiled beans and barley and in parts of southern Mexico the name is used for a corn gruel.)

There is plain, everyday *pozole* which uses the pig's head, feet, and sometimes tail as well. There is also *pozole de lujo;* this deluxe version adds pork loin and chicken.

The following recipe is from the Delgadillo family of Guadalajara, as adapted to stateside cooking by Lilia Delgadillo Bane.

2 pig's feet, split
1 pound fresh pork hock or loin
2 large cloves garlic
1 large onion, sliced
1 bay leaf
4 quarts water
3 pounds chicken parts
2 large cans (29 oz. each) hominy
   Pinch baking soda
3½ teaspoons salt
   Pepper to taste
   Garnish: chopped lettuce, onions, radishes, lime wedges, cheese and crumbled oregano

1. Simmer the pork meats, garlic, onion and bay leaf in water for 1 hour.

2. Add chicken pieces, continue cooking until almost tender, about 1 hour.

3. Add drained hominy, pinch of baking soda, salt and pepper. Cook for 30 minutes.

4. Serve in large bowls with an assortment of chopped lettuce, onions, radishes, lime wedges, cheese and crumbled oregano.

Salsa

The following *very* hot and delicious *salsa* is intended to accompany this *pozole,* or you can serve chopped fresh or canned hot chiles.

10 to 12 *chiles de arbol,* ground
 1 small onion, finely chopped
   Pinch powdered cumin
   Pinch powdered thyme
   Salt and pepper to taste

Lightly fry all the ingredients in a small amount of oil; do not allow to burn. Place in a bowl for serving with the *pozole.* Serves 12.

Caldo de Pollo a la Enedina

(Enedina's chicken soup)

Señorita Enedina Gomez prepared this soup for us in Puerto Vallarta. Note that she leaves the scrubbed feet on the chicken to make her stock.

Chicken feet and duck feet are still valued highly in both Mexican and Chinese cooking. Used in any chicken broth, the feet add flavor and body and are particularly rich in gelatin.

1 large chicken, 3½ to 4 pounds (with feet, if possible)
1 onion
   Salt to taste
3 large *chayotes*
8 small carrots
5 zucchini cut in large chunks
3 large ears of corn, each cut into three pieces
   Lime wedges

1. Wash chicken well and place in a large pot. Cover chicken with water, add onion and salt. Cook until tender.

2. In another pot, cook *chayotes* and carrots in salted water, until almost tender. Add zucchini and corn, and cook until done. Drain vegetables. Peel *chayotes* and cut in large chunks. Keep warm. Cut chicken in serving size pieces. Discard feet.

3. In each bowl place 1 piece of chicken and a piece of each of the vegetables. Add hot chicken broth. Serve with lime wedges and hot *tortillas.* Serves 8.

Sopa de Frijoles

(Bean soup)

2 medium tomatoes, peeled
1 onion, quartered
1 clove garlic
3 tablespoons butter or margarine
4 cups cooked pinto beans (or 2 cans, 16 oz. each)
2 cups chicken broth
1 tablespoon mild powdered chile
   Salt
3 ounces Monterey jack or Muenster cheese, in small cubes
4 strips bacon, fried crisp and crumbled

1. Combine tomatoes, onion and garlic in blender and blend until smooth. Melt butter in a large, heavy saucepan, add tomato mixture and cook over high heat for about 5 minutes.

2. Blend beans and liquid from cooking in blender until smoothly puréed. Add beans to tomato mixture and cook for 5 minutes over medium heat, stirring occasionally.

3. Add chicken broth, chile powder, and salt to taste, and simmer for another 10 to 15 minutes.

4. To serve, place a few cubes of cheese in each bowl. Pour hot soup into bowl and sprinkle with crumbled bacon. Serves 6 to 8.

Sopa de Tortilla

(*Tortilla* soup)

6 to 12 *tortillas,* cut into ¼-inch strips
   Lard or oil for frying, ¼ inch deep
1 tablespoon lard or oil
½ cup chopped onion
2 cloves garlic, crushed
1 can (28 oz.) solid pack tomatoes, puréed in a blender
4 cups chicken stock (or canned chicken broth)
   Salt to taste
   Garnishes: a few fresh cilantro leaves to taste, slightly chopped, grated mild cheddar cheese or grated Monterey jack cheese

1. Fry *tortilla* strips in hot oil (425 degrees) until hardened but not browned. Drain on paper towels and set aside.

Vegetable slices are added to the pot according to their cooking time.

2. In a large pot, heat tablespoon lard or oil, add onion and garlic; cook only until onion is transparent. Add puréed tomatoes, chicken stock and bring to a boil. Reduce heat and simmer for 5 minutes. Add cilantro leaves and salt to taste if desired.

3. To serve: In the bottom of each serving bowl, place a handful of the prepared *tortilla* strips. Ladle the soup over the *tortilla* strips and top with grated cheese. Serves 8.

Sopa de Lima
(Lime soup)

Strictly translated we would have to call this lemon soup in English, but we will be inconsistent in this case. In Yucatan where this recipe originates it is made from Yucatecan *limas agrias,* which translates as sour lemons. Some Mexican recipes suggest using one sour lime and one sweet lemon to approximate the taste; another suggests adding some grapefruit rind. We think it's great with limes.

Lard or oil, ¼ inch deep for frying
Salt
6 to 8 corn *tortillas,* cut into wedges
4 chicken breasts
10 cups chicken broth
1 onion, peeled and quartered
3 cloves garlic, peeled and sliced
6 peppercorns
2 teaspoons salt
½ teaspoon thyme
1 tablespoon lard
½ onion, chopped
1 large, mild, green chile, seeded and chopped (do not roast)
2 tomatoes, chopped
6 limes
⅓ cup cilantro leaves
2 avocados, peeled and sliced

1. Heat the lard or oil to 400 degrees. Lightly salt the *tortilla* wedges and fry until crisp. If made in advance, reheat in a 350 degree oven before adding to the soup. Drain the wedges on paper toweling.

Meat, vegetables and soup courses, all in one dish, with hot bolillos (rolls) *or tortillas. Caldo de Pollo a la Enedina makes a meal.*

Albóndigas *simply means meatballs, but in Mexico, it's almost always meatball soup.*

1. Mix all the ingredients except the tomato sauce, which should be added last, using only enough to make the mixture moist, but firm enough to hold together as balls.

2. Form small meatballs. Moisten your hands frequently with cold water while forming the balls to prevent the meat from sticking.

Caldo (Broth)

½ **small onion, chopped**
1 **clove garlic, minced**
1 **tablespoon bell pepper, minced**
1 **tablespoon oil**
6 **cups beef or chicken stock (or water)**
½ **cup tomato sauce**
½ **teaspoon salt, or to taste**
   Diced or chopped vegetables, raw carrots, Italian or summer squash, celery (optional)

1. Sauté the onion, garlic, and bell pepper in oil until they are soft. Add the stock (or water), tomato sauce and salt, and bring to a hard boil.

2. Add all the meatballs slowly so that the boiling does not stop. If water is used instead of stock, the meatballs will form an adequate stock of their own as they cook. Skim, if necessary.

3. Add the diced or chopped vegetables, as desired. Lower heat to a simmer. Cover and cook for about 25 minutes. Serves 6 to 8.

Besides the hot chile *salsa,* many people enjoy this soup topped with minced cilantro.

Like so many stews and soups, *albóndigas* are best prepared a day in advance of need, especially if water is used instead of stock. They freeze very well.

Menudo Sonorense
(Sonora style tripe soup)

To hear Mexicans talk of the beneficial effects of *menudo,* one would expect to find it included in the pharmacopoeia, along with other medicines and remedies, instead of in a cookbook. It has a reputation for fighting the effects of the *cruda,* the hangover.

2 **or 3 calf's feet, or 2 veal knuckles**
6 **quarts water**
3 **cups** *nixtamal* **or hominy**
5 **or 6 pounds tripe**
3 **onions, chopped**
3 **or 4 cloves garlic, minced**
   Chiles, optional
   Salt and pepper to taste

1. Wash and split calf's feet and precook for one hour.

2. If *nixtamal* is used, be sure to wash it several times to remove the lime which was used in soaking. Precook with the calf's feet.

3. Wash tripe extremely well and cut into bite-size pieces. Add tripe,

2. Place in a soup pot the chicken breasts, broth, quartered onion, garlic slices, peppercorns, salt and thyme. Bring to a boil, reduce heat to simmer, cover and cook 30 minutes. Allow chicken to cool in the broth.

3. Remove chicken; skin and bone the chicken, then shred the meat. Strain the broth into a separate container.

4. Melt 1 tablespoon lard in the soup pot. Add the chopped onion and chile and cook until soft. Add the tomatoes and cook again briefly only until soft.

5. Return the broth to the soup pot and bring to a boil. Add the juice of 3 or 4 fresh limes, plus a squeezed lime half. Reduce heat and simmer 20 minutes.

6. Remove the lime half and add the shredded chicken and cilantro. Simmer an additional 10 minutes.

7. Peel and slice the avocados and cut the remaining limes into wedges. Serve the soup and drop hot *tortilla* sections into each bowl. Have available for individual garnish the sliced avocado and lime wedges. Serves 8.

Sopa de Albóndigas
(Meatball soup)

In Spanish *albóndigas* means meatballs, but in Mexico it most often refers to a soup in which meatballs are the main ingredient. To us, the meatballs must have the distinctive flavor of *yerba buena* (mint) because that was typical at home. This recipe does not include chile, but there should be a bowl of hot *salsa* on the table.

Albóndigas
(Meatballs)

1 **pound lean ground beef**
½ **small onion, minced**
2 **tablespoons bread crumbs**
1 **tablespoon fresh mint, minced** **(or 1 teaspoon crushed dried mint)**
1 **egg, slightly beaten**
1 **teaspoon salt**
⅛ **teaspoon cumin powder**
¼ **teaspoon ground pepper**
2 **tablespoons raw rice**
¼ **cup tomato sauce**

chopped onions, and garlic to the pre-cooked calf's feet and *nixtamal*. If desired, add several washed and seeded dried *ancho, mulato,* or *pasilla* chiles along with the onions and garlic.

4. Simmer for 6 or 7 hours or until the meat and *nixtamal* are tender. Salt and pepper to taste near the end of the cooking time. Remove chiles.

5. Serve piping hot topped with chopped green onion and a pinch per bowl of crushed dry oregano. There should be a bowl of hot *salsa* at hand. *Menudo* wouldn't be authentic without it.

Note: *Nixtamal* can be bought at *tortilla* factories. It is dry corn that has been boiled and soaked in lime water to remove the skins. Dry hominy can be substituted. If only canned hominy is available, add during the last hour of cooking. Serves 10.

Sopa de Fideo
(Vermicelli soup)

12 ounces coiled vermicelli or other pasta
¼ cup oil
½ onion, chopped
1 clove garlic, minced
1 tablespoon bell pepper, chopped
1 tomato, peeled and chopped (or 3 oz. tomato sauce)
2 quarts beef or chicken stock, heated Salt and pepper to taste
4 ounces Monterey jack cheese, in small cubes

1. Brown the vermicelli lightly in the hot oil but be careful not to allow it to burn. Drain excess oil.

2. Add the onion, garlic, bell pepper and tomato; continue to cook until the onion is soft.

3. Add the hot stock and season to taste. Simmer until the vermicelli is tender, about 10 minutes.

4. Add cheese or put a few cubes into each bowl and serve piping hot. Serves 6 to 8.

Sopa de Papas con Chile Verde y Queso
(Potato soup with green chile and cheese)

2 green onions, or ½ small onion, chopped
1 clove garlic, minced
3 *poblano* chiles, roasted, peeled, cleaned and chopped (or use canned mild chiles)
1 tablespoon oil
1 medium tomato (or equivalent in canned whole tomato, chopped)
1 quart beef or chicken stock, heated
3 medium potatoes, cubed A generous pinch of dry oregano Salt and pepper to taste
3 or 4 ounces grated jack cheese

1. Sauté the onion, garlic, and chile in the oil until the onion is soft. Add the tomato and simmer several minutes.

2. Add the hot stock and the potatoes. When the potatoes are tender, add the oregano, salt, pepper and the grated cheese.

3. Serve hot. Serves 4 to 6.

Pozole comes in various styles. Adding your own garnishes makes it a "soup to salad" meal. (See recipe, page 44.)

Sopa Seca de Fideo: *a convenient way to crumble vermicelli is to roll the unopened package with a rolling pin.*

Because the vermicelli scorches easily, stir it constantly while browning in oil.

Sopas secas

Mexican meals often include *sopas secas* or dry soups. They may be rice, any of the various pastas, or even pieces of corn *tortillas*. They are prepared to be served without a broth or liquid, to accompany the main course of a meal. The rice which is almost invariably served with meals at Mexican restaurants is a *sopa seca*. The variations are unlimited and, with the addition of chicken, shrimp, pork or other meats, plus vegetables, *sopas secas* can become a main course.

Sopa de Arroz
(Mexican rice)

This is the most typical *sopa seca*. A Mexican cook's reputation often rests on the consistent good quality of this daily dish. It is almost as common to meals as the inevitable beans.

 1 cup long grain rice
 3 tablespoons oil
 ½ small onion, finely chopped
 1 clove garlic, minced
 1 small tomato, peeled and chopped
  (or 3 ounces tomato sauce)
 ¼ cup fresh or frozen peas
  diced carrots, or green beans
  (optional)
 2 cups boiling chicken stock
 1 teaspoon salt

1. Sauté the washed, drained rice in the hot oil until golden but not brown.

2. Add the onion, garlic, fresh tomato (if used) and any vegetables, and cook slightly.

3. Add the boiling stock, salt, and tomato sauce, if substituted for fresh tomato. Return to a boil, then lower heat, cover, and cook on low heat until the rice is tender and the liquid has been absorbed (22 to 25 minutes).

4. Toss lightly with a fork before serving. Serves 4 to 6.

Arroz Gualdo
(Yellow rice)

This rice, colored and delicately flavored with *achiote*, is typical of Yucatán. *Achiote*, the small, brick-red seeds of the annatto tree, imparts a bright yellow color to the rice and is especially tasty and attractive with fish dishes.

 1½ tablespoons *achiote* (annatto seeds)
 3 tablespoons oil
 1 cup long grain rice
 ½ small onion, chopped
 1 clove garlic, minced
 2 cups chicken stock or water
 1 teaspoon salt

1. Fry the *achiote* in the oil over low heat. Remove the seeds from the oil when they are dark brown, and discard. The oil will be dark orange in color.

2. Add the washed, drained rice to the oil and sauté for about 5 minutes. Add the onion and garlic and cook until it is tender.

3. Add the boiling stock and salt.

Large white corn kernels are sold for making the hominy used in preparing pozole.

Push browned vermicelli to one side of skillet and cook onions, garlic, green pepper and tomatoes.

After vegetables have cooked, mix together, add boiling stock, cover, and steam until liquid is absorbed.

Bring mixture to a boil, lower the flame, cover, and cook for 22 to 25 minutes until the liquid is absorbed. Serves 4 to 6.

Arroz Blanco
(White rice)

3 tablespoons lard or oil
1 clove garlic
1 cup long grain rice
1 small onion, diced
1 teaspoon salt
2½ cups chicken broth

1. In a skillet, melt lard and add garlic. Toast the garlic to a golden brown and remove.

2. Lightly fry rice in hot oil (do not brown). Add onion and salt. Cook until onion is limp.

3. Add chicken broth all at once. Bring to boil, cover and cook over medium heat until all liquid has been absorbed, approximately 35 minutes. Serves 4 to 6.

Arroz Verde
(Green rice)

2 *poblano* chiles, roasted, peeled and cleaned
½ cup fresh cilantro
2½ cups chicken broth
3 tablespoons lard or oil
1 cup long grain rice
½ onion, chopped
1 clove garlic, crushed

1. Place the chiles and cilantro in the blender with ½ cup of the chicken stock. Blend to a purée.

2. In a skillet, heat the lard or oil,

add the rice and cook, stirring constantly, until puffed and golden.

3. Add the onion and garlic and cook until the onion is soft. Add the chile purée and cook briefly.

4. Pour in remaining chicken stock all at once. Bring to a boil, cover and reduce heat to medium. Cook until all liquid has been absorbed, approximately 35 minutes. Toss and serve. Serves 6.

Sopa Seca de Fideo
(Dry soup of vermicelli)
Though not usual in restaurants, this is a common *sopa seca* in private homes in place of rice.

1 package (8 oz.) coiled vermicelli, broken
3 tablespoons oil
½ small onion, finely chopped
1 clove garlic, minced
1 tablespoon chopped bell pepper
1 tomato, peeled and chopped (or 3 oz. tomato sauce)
2 cups beef or chicken stock
Salt and pepper to taste
Parmesan cheese
Sour cream

1. Break the vermicelli in short lengths, then brown in hot oil. It is more delicate than rice; do not burn. Drain excess oil.

2. Push the vermicelli to one side, add onion, garlic, bell pepper and cook until onion is soft. Add tomato and mix all together with the vermicelli.

3. Add the boiling stock and season

to taste. Cover and cook over a very low flame until the liquid is almost completely absorbed.

4. Serve with a sprinkling of grated Parmesan cheese or a dab of sour cream. Serves 4 to 6.

Variation: Other pastas of the noodle family serve equally well. For instance, alphabet pasta may be substituted for the vermicelli. Increase the liquid to 2½ cups. For a delicious liquid soup add 4 to 5 cups of broth.

Lentejas
(Lentils)

1½ cups lentils
4 cups water
1½ teaspoons salt
2 carrots, diced
2 tablespoons lard or oil
½ onion, chopped
2 cloves garlic, crushed
1 tomato, chopped
Salt to taste
Sour cream

1. Wash lentils and place together in a pot with the water, salt and carrots. Bring to a boil, cover and lower heat to simmer for 45 minutes.

2. In a skillet, heat the lard or oil, add the onion and garlic and cook until soft.

3. Add lentils and tomato, cook over medium-high heat for approximately 20 minutes, stirring frequently. Allow lentils to cook down into a paste. Salt to taste. Garnish with sour cream. Serves 6.

Meats and stews

In Mexico, as elsewhere, the tenderest cuts of meat are usually grilled in the most straightforward manner, but great ingenuity is displayed in the preparation of those less tender but often more flavorful cuts.

Traditional Mexican methods of cooking meat are often designed for a cut of meat from an animal that has done a bit of walking around. Returning tourists never seem to compliment the tender succulent *lomo de cerdo* (pork loin) they had, but they do complain about the gorgeous thick steak they were served and couldn't get a fork into. Much of this stems from the Mexican effort to give the tourists what they want, so steaks are offered, often without regard to the suitability of the cut.

It is our impression that there has been a rather rapid improvement in beef quality in the last two or three years, and many friends we've questioned seem to agree. This may be due to the increased use of feedlot procedures, at least for first-class restaurant meat. It may also be that government programs to introduce better breeding stock are beginning to have results in the meat market.

In Mexico the entire animal is still expected to serve the table. Not eating the innards has apparently developed in the U.S. as a byproduct of abundance coupled with a surfeit of delicacy. Clearly our sensibilities do us no credit in this matter; our spectrum of choices is restricted and our nourishment curtailed.

Meat cutters in Mexico traditionally slice with the grain; steaks cut across the grain are recent innovations. This "with the grain" method of cutting meat has excellent logic, considering the methods traditionally used to preserve meat and to prepare

◁

Meat market in Acaxochitlán, Hildalgo uses colonial brass balances to weigh out meat.

it for the table. Since meat is used in many Mexican dishes merely as a savory addition, much as it's used in Chinese cooking, and since refrigeration is not universally available, it is generally bought in small quantities. If the meat is to be shredded, as it often is in Mexican recipes, it is easier to shred a thin small piece when the grain runs the length rather than the depth of the piece.

Cecina

The usefulness of cutting meat *with* the grain can also be seen in making *cecina*. Developed long before the advent of refrigeration, *cecina* is the Mexican cousin of north-of-the-border jerky. Like jerky, it was first employed to preserve meat for those times when fresh meat was not available. Like many other early methods of preserving (from sauerkraut to country ham), it provides some flavor bonuses that promise to keep it around for a long time, in spite of all the newer, more sophisticated methods of food preservation.

Cecina must be cut from a lean chunk of beef, such as flank steak, brisket, or rump. Cutting with the grain, make thin slices about ¼ inch apart. These slices should almost cut through the meat. Make them alternately on opposite sides so that hinges are left between the slices and, when you are done, the meat will open like a folding door. Lightly salt the elongated steak, refold, and allow to sit for half a day.

Next, hang the steak in the sun (3 hours or so in dry weather) until it is surface-dry, but not stiff. When dry, coat it with lemon or lime juice and crushed black pepper. Now

rehang it in the shade for two or three days or until thoroughly dry. Cover it with cheese-cloth to protect it from insects and bring it in at night to protect it from dampness.

Cecina is not only used as dried beef but it is also served before it is fully dried as a thin steak with a fine, aged flavor. *Cecina* may be broiled or barbecued during the first 24 hours of hanging (assuming it's a reasonably tender cut of meat). It should be coated with oil and broiled quickly, using fairly high heat; overcooking will toughen it. The meat can be used at any time for stews; the fully dried meat makes an almost instant beef broth with a flavor that we find exceptionally tasty. Try to preserve some of it for a high protein, lightweight snack for backpacking and for *machaca*. You can store it in a cool, dry, well-ventilated place for a short time. Freeze for long storage.

Machaca

The most important *cecina* dish gets its name from the Spanish verb *machacar,* "to batter or crush." This

New breeding stock seen even on remote rancheros may account for improvements in beef quality.

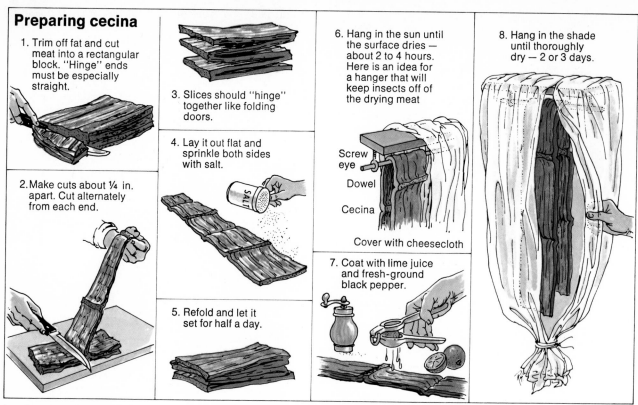

Preparing cecina

1. Trim off fat and cut meat into a rectangular block. "Hinge" ends must be especially straight.

2. Make cuts about ¼ in. apart. Cut alternately from each end.

3. Slices should "hinge" together like folding doors.

4. Lay it out flat and sprinkle both sides with salt.

5. Refold and let it set for half a day.

6. Hang in the sun until the surface dries — about 2 to 4 hours. Here is an idea for a hanger that will keep insects off of the drying meat

Screw eye

Dowel

Cecina

Cover with cheesecloth

7. Coat with lime juice and fresh-ground black pepper.

8. Hang in the shade until thoroughly dry — 2 or 3 days.

is, of course, the method by which the meat is shredded for cooking.

To prepare *machaca*, roast *cecina* under the broiler for a few minutes on both sides until hot and bubbly; cool and shred the meat thoroughly by pounding it on a heavy chopping block. (Mexican cooks pound with a heavy rock.) Or, shred in small amounts in the blender until fluffy. *Machaca* will be more tender if the fluffed meat is dried 10 or 15 minutes in a 200 degree oven before proceeding with the recipe.

We have been told by an old-timer in Sonora that, "*Machaca* made of beef is good and venison is still better; but burro is best of all." We're not at all sure that he was joking, although he laughed when he said it.

The *machaca* that appears on restaurant menus may be the real sundried article, but very often it is made of shredded boiled beef that has been crisped by frying in lard. This can be delicious when seasoned well but it doesn't have the special flavor of the real thing.

Machaca con Huevos
(*Machaca* with eggs)

- 1 tablespoons lard or oil
- ½ cup chopped onion
- 2 tomatoes, peeled and chopped
- 1 or 2 *jalapeño* chiles, seeded and deveined, and chopped (or ¼ cup canned green chiles, chopped)
- 2 cups shredded *machaca*
- 1 cup water
- 2 eggs, beaten
- *Tortillas*
- Grated cheese

1. Heat lard. Sauté onions until tender. Add tomatoes and chiles and cook a few minutes.

2. Add *machaca*, stir until brown and nearly dry.

3. Add water; cook until thick.

4. Add beaten eggs and stir until set.

5. Serve with flour *tortillas*.
Makes 4 servings.

Rollo de Filete
(Stuffed flank steak)

- 1 flank steak, about 1½ pounds
  Vinegar, salt and pepper
- 2 eggs
- 3 canned pimientos, cut in strips
- 2 Anaheim chiles, roasted, peeled, cleaned and cut in strips
- ⅓ cup pine nuts, lightly toasted
- 2 tablespoons oil
- 1 tablespoon chopped onion
- 1 small clove garlic, minced
- 1 tablespoon flour
- 1 teaspoon *ancho* chile, powdered
- 2 cups beef broth
  Chopped parsley

1. Open the steak by splitting it to form two "pages," leaving a hinge so that you have a single extended steak that covers twice the area of the original. This cut should be made in such a direction that the cutting edge of the knife is moving parallel to the grain of the meat.

2. Season the meat with a little vinegar, salt and pepper.

3. Beat the eggs and make a thin omelet. Cut into strips. Arrange the strips of egg, pimiento and chiles alternately over the extended meat, parallel to the grain.

4. Roll the meat so the grain runs the length of the roll and tie securely in several places with string.

5. Toast the pine nuts lightly in a shallow pan in a low oven.

6. Heat oil, fry the rolled meat on all sides until brown. Remove to a baking pan.

7. Add the onion and garlic to the drippings in the frying pan, and cook a few minutes. Add flour and powdered chile, cook 2 minutes. Add broth and mix well. Place the pine nuts in the blender (be sure pine nuts have cooled), blend, then add the broth mixture and blend until very smooth. Return to pan and cook over low heat for 5 minutes to thicken.

8. Pour sauce over the rolled meat and bake, basting occasionally, in a 350 degree oven for 1 hour for medium rare or 1½ hours for well done. Top with chopped parsley. Serves 4 to 6.

Birria

Birria is a traditional hole-in-the-ground dish like *barbacoa* or pit cooking, and is still cooked for country celebrations in this way. Usually a whole lamb is cooked.

This recipe was given to us by Señora Victoria Quintero García. It is an authentic hole-in-the-ground version that we have tested and modified for oven cooking with some helpful advice given to us by Marcos Armas.

The object of the game is to keep escaping steam to a minimum to prevent its stealing any of the flavor. Since *birria* is cooked in a pot, this would seem simple. But since there is naturally more steam in a well-sealed hole in the ground than there is in your oven, it was necessary to make a few modifications. We put a low rack in the bottom of the cooking pan and added a bit of water. Of course, we sealed the lid with *masa,* as is traditional, but we decided to double seal it as well. We also used an alternate method of sealing that is recommended in Josefina Velazquez de Leon's *Mexican Cookbook.* This consists of putting a layer of parchment over the meat and covering with a layer of *masa.*

Oven Birria

2½ cups white vinegar
2 tablespoons sugar
1 teaspoon salt
3 pounds lamb shank
2 pounds pork loin ribs

Combine the vinegar, sugar and salt. Marinate the meat in this mixture for 2 hours.

Chile mixture

6 dried *pasilla* chiles
1½ cups vinegar from meat marinade
1 teaspoon oregano
10 peppercorns
1 small clove garlic
Dash of cumin
1 small bay leaf
1 cup water
***Masa* to seal the pot**

1. Lightly toast the chiles; remove the seeds and veins. Cook the chiles in the 1½ cups vinegar mixture until soft.

2. Combine chiles, vinegar, oregano, peppercorns, garlic and cumin into a smooth paste using a blender or *molcajete.* Add more vinegar if necessary, to have a sauce of medium consistency.

3. Coat the lamb and pork thoroughly with the chile mixture and place on a rack in a deep 10-inch pot with a lid. Add the bay leaf and 1 cup of water.

4. Cover the meat with parchment paper and seal tightly with a layer of *masa.* Place the lid on the pot and seal again with more *masa* around the lid.

5. Cook in a 350 degree oven for 4 hours.

Sauce

1 dried *ancho* chile
2 large tomatoes
Chopped raw onion for garnish

1. Remove the seeds and veins from the *ancho* chile.

2. Half cover the tomatoes with water and cook with the chile until soft.

3. Purée the tomatoes and chile in the blender. Strain.

At the end of the cooking time, remove the lid of *masa* from the meat and discard. Skim off the fat from the pan drippings. Add the strained tomato sauce to the remaining drippings and mix well.

Serve the meat with the sauce and garnish with the chopped onion. The meat will be succulent and falling off the bones. Goat, mutton or veal may also be used. Serves 8.

Carne al Pastor
(Meat, shepherd style)

Another way to use meat cut with the grain is to cook it vertically on the ingenious charcoal barbecue made especially for *carne al pastor,* sold at stands. Thin steaks cut along the grain are impaled in a circular, staggered arrangement on a single spindle with a supporting disk at the bottom. This stacked pyramid of meat may be as large as a leg of beef.

The spindle of meat is suspended in front of a vertical charcoal fire stacked in a "fireplace" behind the spindle. As the spindle is turned slowly before the fire, the cooked meat is trimmed off. The trimming quickly turns the stack into a smooth, tapered cylinder.

Repeated vertical knife cuts are made in this cylinder to control the size of the pieces of meat that are trimmed off. The cooked surface peels away in a cascade of small pieces, each roughly a quarter inch square. Each succulent particle that falls away in the cutting is like a miniature roast beef, with one seared surface and one succulent one. (It is easy to see that this whole procedure would be nearly impossible if the grain of the meat slices didn't run at right angles to the spindle so that the final cutting is across the grain.)

The juicy tidbits of meat are scooped into a small *tortilla,* often an overlapping pair, and rolled up. The customer then adds chopped onions, tomatoes, cilantro, and a choice of *salsas* to taste. This is an ingeniously efficient way to serve freshly cooked meat over an extended time period.

Layers of thinly sliced beef are spindled and revolved before a charcoal fire. This way the cooked surface can be sliced away and served as fast as it cooks.

At some stands, the meat slices are marinated in a sauce before barbecuing, but generally they are only salted. While this technique is far from practical for most U.S. cooks, *carne al pastor* would be a great party attraction.

Cecina en adobo

Pork is also cut and served as *cecina*, but generally as "*cecina en adobo*." In most cases, when ordered in a restaurant, the pork slices have simply marinated a short time in the *adobo* sauce. *Adobo,* a paste primarily of chiles, usually with vinegar, salt, garlic, and oregano, was originally a means of pickling and preserving meat. The coating of chile paste not only kept the fat from becoming rancid but also discouraged the family dog and local coyotes.

Since the *adobos* you may use as a marinade are likely to vary greatly in hotness they will also vary in their preservative properties.

Puerco en Adobo
(Pork marinated in red chile paste)

---

5 dried *ancho* chiles
3 dried Anaheim chiles
2 dried *pasilla* chiles
4 cloves garlic, minced
½ teaspoon oregano
¼ teaspoon ground cumin
1 tablespoon salt
½ cup white wine vinegar
4 pounds pork (8 pork steaks or a
** 4-pound pork shoulder or butt roast**
** cut into 8 steaks)**
Optional garnishes: sour cream, sliced
** avocado, thinly sliced white onion,**
** radish slices, *salsa verde***
** (See page 27)**

1. Warm the chiles on the *comal* or frying pan to soften; do not toast.

Discard the stems and some seeds.

2. Place the chiles in a saucepan and weight them down with a small plate. Add water only to cover the chiles. Bring to a boil and cook for 5 minutes. Set aside for 2 hours. Drain the chiles; remove most of the peel.

3. Place the chile pulp and seeds in the blender together with the garlic, oregano, cumin, salt and vinegar. Blend to a textured purée.

4. Spread the chile paste over both sides of the meat and rub in well. Cover the meat loosely with waxed paper and allow to season in refrigerator for 1 to 3 days.

5. Barbecue or broil. Garnish and serve. Serves 8.

Dona Maria splits pig feet for Patas de Cerdo en Escabeche.

Sauce begins with onions and tomatoes cooked in oil.

Raw Mexican sugar, here as Piloncillos, is an essential part of the sauce.

After separating yolks, whip egg whites until foamy but not stiff.

Drain and thoroughly dry the pig's feet before sprinkling with flour.

Fry gently in medium-hot oil until golden brown. Drain on paper towels.

Patas de Cerdo *is best served in large deep bowls with plenty of hot* tortillas.

Lomo en Salsa de Almendras
(Pork loin in almond sauce)

2 pounds pork loin steaks
  Lard or oil for frying
1 pound tomatoes, finely chopped
2 medium onions, finely chopped
8 ounces ground almonds
1 teaspoon salt
¼ teaspoon pepper

1. Sauté the meat in lard or oil. Arrange in a baking dish.

2. Mix the rest of the ingredients. Pour over the meat.

3. Cook for 40 minutes at 350 degrees or until done. Serves 8.

Patas de Cerdo en Escabeche
(Pig's feet in *escabeche*)

This recipe is from Doña María Garcia Quintero of Puerto Vallarta. It is prepared with pig's feet but would also be delicious with cuts of pork, or even with chicken breasts.

4 pig's feet (about 3 pounds), well
  washed, split, and cut across in
  approximately 3-inch pieces
1 teaspoon salt

Cover pig's feet with water, add salt. Bring to a boil, simmer until tender (about 2 hours for small pig's feet), or cook in pressure cooker. Drain and dry well.

Sauce

¼ cup oil
1¼ cup onion, finely chopped
4 large tomatoes, peeled and
  chopped, or 3 cups canned tomatoes
4 tablespoons sesame seeds
1 cup dark brown sugar
1 cinnamon stick
2½ cups water
½ cup vinegar

Heat oil in a large pot. Add onion and cook until soft. Add tomatoes and fry a few minutes. Add rest of ingredients and cook for 30 minutes.

Batter

6 eggs, separated
½ teaspoon salt
1 cup oil
  Flour

1. Sprinkle egg whites with a little cold water. Whip until very foamy but not stiff. Add beaten yolks and salt. Continue beating until well mixed.

2. Heat 1 cup oil in heavy, deep frying pan. Sprinkle pig's feet with flour, dip in batter, and fry in oil until golden. Drain on paper towels.

Arrange pig's feet in a serving dish and pour the sauce over them. Serve hot with *tortillas* and refried beans. Serves 6 to 8.

Ropa Vieja
("Old clothes")

In spite of its unusual name, variations of *ropa vieja* are common in most Mexican households. This recipe is very similar to many served under the more appealing name of *machaca* in Southern California restaurants. These are made with shredded meat rather than with the authentic *machacas* made with pounded dried beef, or *cecina*. This is an excellent filling for *burritos*.

1 pound beef chuck
1 medium onion, chopped
2 tablespoons oil
3 tomatoes, chopped
3 *serrano* or *jalapeño* chiles, fresh
  or canned, seeded and chopped
  Salt
3 eggs, beaten

1. Cook the meat in salted water until tender. Drain, and shred the meat after it cools.

2. Sauté the onions in the oil until tender. Add the tomatoes and chiles and continue to cook. Mix in the shredded meat and season to taste.

3. Lower the heat and add the beaten eggs. Stir sufficiently to keep the egg from forming an omelet. Serve with hot *tortillas*. Makes 4 servings as a stew, 8 to 10 as a filling for *tacos* or *burritos*.

Albóndigas en Mole Verde
(Meatballs in green *mole*)

½ pound lean ground beef
½ pound ground pork
½ slice bread
½ teaspoon mint leaves, chopped
⅛ teaspoon pepper
⅛ teaspoon cumin powder
½ teaspoon salt
1 egg

Mix all the ingredients. Form small meatballs. (Moisten hands with cold water to keep the meat from sticking to them.)

Mole sauce

1 can (10 oz.) *tomatillos*, drained
1 lettuce leaf
2 *serrano* chiles, chopped
2 sprigs cilantro
½ onion
2 tablespoons lard or oil
3 cups beef stock

1. Blend the first five ingredients in a blender.

2. Heat the lard or oil. Fry blended vegetables, stirring to keep them from burning.

3. Add stock and mix well. When sauce begins to boil, add meatballs slowly so that boiling continues. Simmer until the meatballs are cooked. Serve hot. Serves 4.

Chile con carne
(Chile with meat)

We present our versions of chile con carne without apology. It's easy to understand why Mexico would wish to disown much of what is called "chile" in the U.S., and it's also easy to understand why Texas and New Mexico are quite willing to annex the dish. Just remember that Mexicans have been cooking all kinds of meat with all kinds of chiles for a long time.

Noemi Quiroga's Chile con Carne
(Chile with meat)

This version of chile with meat is about as basic as you can get, and if the beef is good and you have a good powdered chile, it's hard to beat. It is also a way to get acquainted with the differences in dried chile flavors. Try this with an *ancho* powder, a *pasilla* powder or a mild New Mexico powder and find out how different chile flavors can be.

3 pounds beef (chuck, brisket or round), cut in large chunks
Water to half cover meat
1 teaspoon salt
¼ teaspoon pepper
2 tablespoon lard
1 to 2 tablespoons flour for thickening
2 or more tablespoons powdered chile

1. Half cover meat with salted water, add pepper and bring to a boil. Lower heat and cook until almost tender, about 1½ hours.

2. Remove meat from broth and cut into bite-size pieces. Reserve broth.

3. Sauté meat in lard, sprinkle with the flour, stir and cook a few minutes. Add powdered chile and 2 to 3 cups of meat broth. Simmer 30 minutes. Serve with refried beans and hot flour *tortillas.* Serves 6.

Chile con Carne y Frijoles
(Chile with meat and beans)

3½ pound chuck roast
4 cups beans (2 cups dried red or pinto beans, cooked and drained)
6 dried *ancho* chiles
2 dried *pasilla* chiles
1 teaspoon dried oregano
½ teaspoon ground cumin
1 can (1 lb.) tomatoes
3 cloves garlic, peeled and chopped
1 tablespoon salt
2 tablespoons lard
1 large onion, chopped
2 cups reserved beef broth
Garnish: crushed chile *pequin* or *Japonés,* to be added individually

1. Cover the meat with cold water, bring to a boil, cover and simmer 3 hours. Reserve broth, coarsely chop or shred the meat.

Real chile con carne *calls for large chunks of cooked beef.*

A simple chile sauce, a Texas and New Mexico favorite, completes the dish.

Served with flour tortillas, Chile Con Carne *is a hearty noon meal.*

2. Cook the beans as for *Frijoles de Olla.* (See page 78.)

3. Toast the chiles well on a griddle preheated over medium heat. Remove the stems and most seeds.

4. Crumble chiles into the blender. Add the oregano and cumin and blend into a fine powder. Add to the blender the tomatoes, garlic and salt. Blend briefly on low speed, just to an even consistency.

5. In a large pot, melt 2 tablespoons lard; cook the onion until soft. Add the chile purée and fry briefly over high heat. Add the chopped meat and cook 5 minutes over medium heat. Stir in 2 cups of the reserved beef broth, bring to a boil, reduce to simmer. Add the 4 cups of drained beans and simmer 40 minutes. Serves 8 to 10.

Chile Verde con Carne de Res
(Green chile with beef)

2 pounds lean beef, cubed
2 tablespoons lard or oil
1 small onion, chopped
2 cloves garlic, minced
1 tomato, peeled and chopped
1 pound fresh, large mild green chiles, roasted, peeled, cleaned and chopped (or 10 canned green chiles, chopped)
2 canned *serrano* chiles seeded, rinsed and finely chopped (use *jalapeño* chiles if hotter taste is desired)
1 tablespoon flour
1 cup water
1 teaspoon salt
⅛ teaspoon pepper

1. Sauté the meat in the lard or oil until tender.

2. Add the onions and garlic and continue to cook until the onion is soft. Add tomato and chiles, and cook for another 10 minutes.

3. Dissolve flour in water and add to the cooled meat and vegetables while stirring. Simmer a short time longer, until meat is thoroughly cooked.

4. Season with salt and pepper and serve hot. Serves 6.

Colas de Buey Chiapas
(Oxtails *chiapas*)

3 pounds oxtails
4 to 6 cups water
3 tablespoons vinegar
1 inch piece of cinnamon
3 cloves garlic
10 whole allspice
3 cloves
1 teaspoon salt
⅛ teaspoon pepper
1 or 2 *chorizos* (sausages)
2 tomatoes, cut up
4 tablespoons *masa harina*

1. Put oxtails in a large pot. Add enough water to half cover. Add vinegar, cinnamon, garlic, allspice, cloves, salt and pepper.

2. Remove skin from the *chorizos* and add to the pot. Cover and cook for about 2½ hours.

3. Add tomatoes and continue cooking for 30 minutes.

4. Half an hour before serving, make a thick paste with some of the liquid and the *masa harina;* add to the pot, stir and cook until thickened. Serve with Mexican rice. Serves 6.

Chile Verde
(Green chile and pork stew)

10 fresh, mild, long green chiles (or canned whole green chiles)
4 pounds pork roast, trimmed and cut into 1-inch cubes
1 onion, coarsely chopped
3 cloves garlic, crushed
½ teaspoon ground cumin
1 teaspoon oregano
3 large tomatoes, peeled and cut into wedges
1 teaspoon salt
½ teaspoon freshly ground black pepper
Sour cream

1. Roast and peel the chiles, tear into strips and set aside. Removal of seeds and veins is optional in this recipe. If canned chiles are used, rinse and tear into strips.

2. Cover meat with cold water, bring to a boil, cover and reduce to simmer, cooking 1 hour. Allow meat to cool in its own broth until easy to handle. Trim fat from meat.

3. Over medium-low heat, render remaining fat from meat and allow meat to brown. Remove meat and drippings from pot.

4. Measure out 2 tablespoons drippings. Sauté onion and garlic in drippings and allow onion to cook soft. Stir in the cumin and oregano. Add the tomatoes and chile strips and allow tomatoes to cook soft. Add meat, salt and pepper.

5. Cover and cook 10 minutes over medium-high heat. Lower to medium-low, uncover and cook an additional 20 minutes. Garnish with sour cream. Serves 8.

Variation: This stew is also made using *tomatillos* rather than red tomatoes. Replace the 3 large tomatoes with 2 cans (10 oz. each) *tomatillos,* drained, or 1 pound fresh *tomatillos,* cooked and drained.

Carne Adobado
(Marinated meat)

This is another recipe from Doña María García Quintero of Puerto Vallarta. It calls for barbecuing the meat but it can be baked or broiled.

8 dried *ancho* chiles or 8 tablespoons mild chile powder
1 cup vinegar
½ Mexican chocolate tablet (or ¼ cup melted chocolate plus dash of cinnamon)
3 cloves
½ teaspoon oregano
2 cloves garlic, crushed or finely chopped
Pinch cumin
2-inch piece of stick cinnamon
½ teaspoon salt
¼ teaspoon pepper
1 large tomato, chopped
2 pounds pork loin with ribs, cut into serving size pieces, or 2 pounds thinly sliced pork chops

1. If using dried chiles, wash, remove seeds and veins and cook in vinegar until soft.

2. Grind chiles in blender.

3. Return ground chiles or chile powder to pan; add chocolate and cook until chocolate is melted.

4. Remove from stove; add remaining ingredients, except meats.

5. Cool. Add meat and marinate overnight.

6. Barbecue over charcoal, basting with sauce until done. Serves 4 to 6.

Guisado
(Pork stew with cactus)

1½ pounds pork steak or chops, cubed
2 tablespoons oil
2 medium onions, chopped
2 cloves garlic, minced
1 teaspoon ground cumin powder
2½ teaspoons salt
1 jar *nopalitos,* rinsed and drained
1 can (7 oz.) mild green chiles, seeded and chopped
8 medium potatoes, peeled and diced

1. Brown the meat well in the oil. Add onions, garlic, cumin, and salt, and continue to cook slowly until the onion is soft but not brown.

2. Add the *nopalitos,* chopped chiles and diced potatoes. Cover and simmer for an hour, adding more water, if necessary.

3. Serve with warm *tortillas.* Serves 8.

Only photographers and livestock wander about the village during siesta.

Chile Verde con Nopalitos
(Pork stew with cactus)

1 pound lean pork steak or chops, in small cubes or strips
2 tablespoons oil or shortening
1 small onion, finely chopped
1 clove garlic, minced
2 cups *tomatillos,* drained with liquid reserved
2 or 3 canned *jalapeño* chiles, rinsed, seeded, and cut into small strips
1 teaspoon salt
Pepper to taste
1 jar (16 to 20 oz.) *nopalitos,* drained and rinsed

1. Brown the meat well in the oil.

2. Add onion, garlic, *tomatillos,* strips of chile, salt, pepper and *nopalitos.* (Add some of the liquid from the *tomatillos* to the meat, if needed.) Simmer for 15 minutes.

3. Serve with rice and *tortillas.* Serves 6.

Guiso de Puerco
(Pork stew)

2 pounds pork roast, cut into 2-inch chunks
1 onion, chopped
2 cloves garlic, crushed
2 cups lentils
1 can (1 lb.) solid pack tomatoes, puréed in blender
⅔ cup raisins
3 tablespoons lard or oil
1 plantain or 1 large, firm, underripe banana, sliced
1 cup pineapple chunks, fresh or canned, drained
1½ teaspoons salt
½ teaspoon pepper
Sour cream for garnish

1. Cover meat chunks with cold water. Bring to a boil, cover and simmer 1 hour. Add onions, garlic, lentils, tomato purée and raisins. (If necessary add more water to cover.) Bring to boil, cover and simmer 1½ hours.

2. In a skillet, heat lard and sauté plantain or banana, and pineapple. Add fruit, salt and pepper to stew and simmer uncovered 10 minutes. Garnish with sour cream. Serves 8.

Orange slices supply moisture that controls the temperature of the lard that cooks the carnitas (little meats).

Nopalitos con Carne de Puerco y Chile Verde
(Cactus with pork and green chile)

1 pound lean pork chop or steak, cut in small cubes or strips
2 tablespoons oil or shortening
1 small onion, chopped
1 clove garlic, minced
2 small tomatoes, peeled, and chopped (or 2 canned tomatoes)
½ teaspoon salt
1 jar (16 to 20 oz.) nopalitos
2 fresh, mild, long green chiles, roasted, peeled, cleaned and chopped or 2 canned green chiles, chopped
2 eggs
1 tablespoon milk
Salt and pepper

1. Brown the meat well in the oil. Add onion, garlic, tomatoes, salt, and sauté a while longer.

2. Rinse the *nopalitos* in cold water and drain well. Add to the meat mixture. Simmer to reduce the liquid. Add the chopped chiles and continue cooking until the mixture is fairly dry.

3. Beat the two eggs with the milk. Add salt and pepper to taste. Spread the meat mixture evenly over the skillet. Pour the beaten egg over the meat. Cook slowly until the egg is set. Serve hot. Serves 6.

Tinga Poblana
(Puebla style stew)

Tingas are stews typical of the area around Puebla, and common throughout central Mexico. The meat may be pork, veal, or chicken. Because the meat is usually shredded, and the chicken fricasseed, this dish is really another version of *Ropa Vieja* (see page 55). It is excellent with hot *tortillas,* or as a topping or filling for one of the *sopes* or other *antojitos*.

Tingas often include *chorizo,* which will dominate both the color and taste. If you enjoy the snappy taste, be sure to sauté *chorizo* and drain excess grease before adding to the other ingredients.

2 pounds pork shoulder
Salt
2 or 3 chorizos (optional)
2 tablespoons lard or oil
1 large onion, finely chopped
1 clove garlic, minced
2 large tomatoes, chopped
2 or 3 canned chipotle chiles, chopped
½ teaspoon oregano
1 avocado, peeled, sliced
1 onion, sliced

1. Cook pork in a little water with salt, covered, until very tender, between 1½ to 2 hours. Drain meat, reserve stock. Shred meat.

2. If *chorizo* is used, skin, sauté and drain away excess grease.

3. Heat lard or oil, add onion and garlic and cook until tender. Add tomatoes, chiles, and oregano and simmer for another 5 minutes.

4. Add the pork (and *chorizo*) with about ¼ cup broth from reserved stock, and salt to taste. Simmer until mixture begins to thicken. Serve with onion and avocado slices. Serves 6 to 8.

Chicharrones en Chile
(Pork rind in chile)

Chiles, 3 serrano, or 3 or 4 güero, or 2 jalapeños, chopped
4 cloves garlic, chopped
3 cans tomatillos (12 oz.) drained (or 1½ lbs. fresh, cooked and drained)
1 tablespoon lard
½ onion, chopped
1 cup water
Pork rinds (5 oz. package), broken into bite-size pieces
⅓ cup cilantro, slightly chopped

1. Place chiles, garlic and *tomatillos* in the blender. Mix briefly.

2. In a large pot, heat the lard and cook the onion until soft. Add the *tomatillo* mixture and the water. Bring to a boil.

3. Add the pork rind pieces and cilantro, reduce heat to simmer, cover and cook for 20 minutes. Serves 4 to 6.

Carnitas
(Little meats)

Though the traditional *carnitas* found throughout Mexico are usually pork, at home we have enjoyed these ''little meats'' prepared from either pork or lamb. Inexpensive cuts may be used. A pork butt or other boned roast serves well.

2 or 3 pounds lard (no substitute)
3½ pounds pork roast, butt or shoulder cut
1 small orange, cut in slices
½ cup cilantro leaves, slightly chopped (optional)

1. Place lard in a heavy, deep pot, over medium-low heat. Trim fat from the meat and cut the meat into 3-inch cubes and lightly salt. (Meat may be cut into 1-inch cubes for use as an appetizer.) When the lard has melted, place the meat, orange slices and cilantro in the pot. (Melted lard should completely cover the meat.)

2. Cook over medium-low heat: 1½ to 2 hours for 1-inch cubes, 2 to 2½ hours for 3-inch cubes. The lard will begin to boil after 30 minutes. The orange slices supply the water which allows the lard to boil. Boil gently through the cooking process. As the water gradually cooks away, the temperature of the lard will rise, allowing the meat to brown. If the meat has not browned at the end of the cooking time, remove the orange slices. Watch carefully and remove the meat as soon as it browns.

3. Drain on paper towels. The *carnitas,* when done, will have a dry, crisp exterior with a moist, succulent interior.

4. To serve, place 1-inch cubes on toothpicks, for dipping in *salsa* or *guacamole.* Serve *carnitas* hot. May be reheated in 350 degree oven for 10 minutes. Serves 6 as appetizers or makes filling for 12 tacos.

Carnitas de Cordero
(Lamb carnitas)

2 or 3 pounds meaty lamb necks, in small sections
1 cup water
1 clove garlic
Salt
1 small bay leaf, or 2 whole cloves, or both
Several whole peppercorns

Carnitas *(small meats)* are cooked crisp on the outside, succulent on the inside. Pick them up *in* a tortilla *and garnish with* salsa, *sour cream, onions and cheese.*

1. Cook the lamb necks in a pressure cooker for 10 minutes with 1 cup water and the other ingredients.

2. Place the meat and remaining liquid in a flat roasting pan or tray. Discard other ingredients.

3. Roast in a 325 degree oven until browned on all sides. Do not allow to burn or dry out too much.

4. Serve with a fresh *salsa* and hot *tortillas.* Serves 2 to 3.

To prepare without a pressure cooker, cook all the ingredients in a covered roasting pan until the meat is tender but some liquid remains. Uncover and continue to cook until the meat is browned to your taste.

Fiambres Surtidos
(Assorted cold meat meal)

Meats

3 fresh pig's feet, cut into 6 pieces each
1 (2 to 3 pounds) beef tongue
3 pounds chicken pieces

Vegetables

1 pound green beans
8 small new potatoes.

1. Place the meats into separate pots, *each* pot containing the following ingredients, cover with cold water.

2 cloves garlic
⅓ onion, cut in large pieces
2 teaspoons salt
⅛ teaspoon thyme
¼ teaspoon oregano (for tongue and pig's feet only)
1 bay leaf
8 peppercorns

2. Bring each pot to a boil, cover and simmer.
2½ hours for pig's feet
2½ hours for beef tongue
30 minutes for chicken

Allow the meats to cool in their own broth until easy to handle. Place the pig's feet in a large bowl. Skin and slice the tongue, skin and bone the chicken pieces. Add the tongue and chicken pieces to the same bowl.

3. Cook green beans and potatoes *(ejotes* and *papas)* and add them to the meats. (See page 76, omitting step 3).

4. Pour the vinaigrette (recipe follows) over all. Allow to marinate at least 4 hours in the refrigerator.

Vinaigrette

2 cloves garlic, minced
¾ cup white wine vinegar
2 teaspoons salt
1 teaspoon pepper
1 tablespoon dry or Dijon mustard
1 cup olive oil
1 cup salad oil
2 tablespoons cilantro leaves, chopped
2 tablespoons capers

Combine all ingredients and shake, or mix briefly in the blender.

Garnishes

Pickled onion rings (see page 77)
Jalapeños en escabeche, filled with cheese, available canned or use crumbled *queso fresco* or feta cheese to fill
whole ripe olives
Radishes, sliced or flowerets
4 hard cooked eggs, sliced
1 head iceberg lettuce, shredded
Salsa de Chipotle (page 27)

To Assemble:

On a large platter, place the shredded lettuce and arrange the meats on top. Place the vegetables around the meats, pour the remaining vinaigrette over all.

Garnish the platter with the olives, radishes and egg slices. Serve the pickled onions and the *jalapeños* in two separate bowls. Accompany this meal with warmed *bolillos* (Mexican dinner rolls), butter, and cold Mexican beer. Serves 8.

Conejo Envinado
(Rabbit in white wine)

¼ cup lard or oil
3 to 4 pound rabbit, cut into serving pieces
3 cloves garlic
1 onion, coarsely chopped
3 *poblano* chiles, roasted, peeled, cleaned and torn into strips *(rajas)*
2 large tomatoes (1 pound), peeled and cut into thin wedges
⅛ teaspoon thyme
1 teaspoon salt
¼ teaspoon pepper
1 cup dry white wine
½ cup chicken broth

1. Melt the lard and brown the rabbit pieces at 370 degrees, 10 minutes each side. Remove the rabbit and set aside.

2. Allow the garlic to toast to a golden brown in the lard. Remove the garlic and add the onions, allowing them to cook until soft.

3. Add the chile *rajas,* tomato wedges, thyme, salt and pepper. Stir several times.

4. Add the wine and broth. Bring to a boil.

5. Add the rabbit pieces, reduce the heat, cover and simmer for 1 to 1½ hours (depending on the size of the rabbit pieces), or until cooked through. Turn the meat at least once while simmering and baste occa-

The waiter cooks and carves your "Tablita Mixta" (mixed grill) over charcoal next to your table in Córdoba, Vera Cruz.

sionally. This recipe works very well in an electric skillet. Serves 6.

Empanadas
(Turnovers)

The *empanada* is common to all Hispanic countries. Brought to the New World by the Spanish, it has spread to many countries and assumed various forms, from tiny dessert *empanaditas,* the size of ravioli, to the *empanada gallega,* a large meat pie big enough for a whole family. Stuffed with seafood or meat and vegetables, it is served hot or cold in slices, and even taken on picnics. The dough varies from place to place and can be anything from an elegant, flaky pastry to a bread dough that will "stick to the ribs."

In Spanish America, the *empanada* is a true turnover, rather than a pie, stuffed with *picadillo* (recipe follows), other meat mixtures and fish. Sweet potatoes, pumpkin, preserves, custard or fruit combinations, are particular favorites during the Christmas season.

Pick your pastry according to whether the *empanada* will be used as a substantial meal item or as a dessert. With the well-stocked frozen

foods section of supermarkets, it is a simple matter to buy very satisfactory premixed doughs, pie crusts, and even flaky pastry. Any can be used with *empanada* recipes. If you prefer to start from scratch, here is a typical pastry recipe.

Pastry

2 cups flour
2 teaspoons baking powder
2 tablespoons sugar (optional)
½ teaspoon salt
⅓ cup shortening
⅓ cup ice water

1. Sift the dry ingredients into a bowl. Sugar may be omitted from dough for meat *empanadas.*

2. Cut in the shortening. Add only enough ice water to hold the dough together.

3. Roll out dough on a slightly floured board to about ⅛-inch thickness. Cut out circles of the size desired, depending on use (6 inches for meat *empanadas* and 3 inches for little dessert or hors d'oeuvres turnovers). Makes 8 to 10 six-inch *empanadas,* about 20 three-inch *empanaditas.*

4. Place filling (recipes follow) on half of each circle, leaving an edge all around. Moisten the edge with water.

The grill and all comes to the table and the meat (beef, pork, sweetbreads and kidneys) stays hot.

2. Add onion and tomato, cook until soft. Add precooked potatoes, the steamed chard and heat through.

3. Cool to handle easily and fill prepared pastry. (See page 60.) Filling for 8 to 10 *empanadas*.

Camarón
(Shrimp filling)

- **2 tablespoons margarine or butter**
- **½ onion, chopped**
- **1½ pounds shrimp, chopped**
- **3 fresh *poblano* chiles, roasted, peeled, seeded and chopped**
- **Salt to taste**

1. In a skillet, melt the margarine and sauté the onion until soft.

2. Add the shrimp, chiles and heat through. Season to taste.

3. Cool to handle easily and fill prepared pastry. Filling for 8 to 10 *empanadas*.

Chorizo
(Mexican sausage)

- **3½ pounds boneless pork shoulder roast**
- **5 dried *ancho* chiles**
- **3 dried *pasilla* chiles**
- **2 to 4 *Japonés* chiles**
- **½ rounded teaspoon ground coriander seed**
- **½ rounded teaspoon dried oregano**
- **½ rounded teaspoon ground cloves**
- **¼ teaspoon cumin seed**
- **1 tablespoon salt**
- **3 tablespoons Hungarian paprika**
- **6 cloves garlic, chopped**
- **¾ cup white wine vinegar**

1. Coarsely grind or finely chop the meat.

2. Toast the *ancho* and *pasilla* chiles well on a preheated *comal* or heavy frying pan over medium heat. Remove the stems and seeds (reserve 2 tablespoons chile seeds). Allow the chiles to cool.

3. Break into pieces and place in the blender. Toast the *Japonés* chiles and the reserved chile seeds. Grind them fine in a blender. Add the coriander, oregano, cloves, cumin, salt and paprika. Blend all to a fine powder. Add the garlic and vinegar. Blend to mix well.

4. Add the chile purée to the chopped meat and work together well with the hands.

5. Cover and refrigerate sausage to season, up to two days. Mix well twice each day.

In a skillet, melt 1 tablespoon lard, add the sausage and cook slowly for 15 to 20 minutes. Then proceed with any recipe calling for *chorizo*. Makes 3½ pounds. (1 cup homemade *chorizo* equals ½ pound.)

Chorizo may be frozen after two days' seasoning.

Press together to seal. Flute the sealed edge. Top may be brushed with butter or beaten egg.

5. Bake on a lightly greased sheet at 400 degrees for 15 to 20 minutes, depending on size. Some cooks prefer them deep fried.

Fillings

Empanada fillings allow for the ingenuity and inventiveness of the cook. Anything is fair game, including game. In Vera Cruz, a common filling is shrimp, but almost any kind of seafood can be used, as well as combinations of any meat with vegetables and spices, chicken or turkey with leftover *mole* sauce. In fact, *empanadas* are an excellent outlet for leftovers of all kinds. For sweet *empanadas,* the most common fillings are pumpkin, sweet potato, with or without pineapple, sweet potato and grated coconut, apple chunks with cinnamon, custards, all varieties of preserves. Use your imagination.

Picadillo

Here is a *picadillo* recipe which is equally good as a filling for *tacos* or for *empanadas.*

- **1 pound lean ground beef (or leftover cooked meat, shredded)**
- **2 tablespoons lard or oil for sautéeing**
- **1 small onion, minced**
- **1 clove garlic, minced**
- **2 medium tomatoes, peeled, seeded and chopped**
- **1 apple, peeled, cored, and chopped**
- **½ cup soup stock or water**
- **¼ cup seedless raisins, plumped in hot water and drained**
- **⅛ teaspoon powdered cinnamon**
- **Pinch ground cloves**
- **Scant pinch ground cumin**
- **Salt and pepper to taste**
- **Oil or shortening (if meat is very lean)**

1. Sauté the meat until brown.

2. Add the onion and garlic and continue cooking until they are soft.

3. Add the remaining ingredients and simmer for 25 minutes until liquid is absorbed. Filling for 8 to 10 6-inch *empanadas.*

Chorizo y Papas
(Sausage and potato filling)

- **1 pound *chorizo***
- **2 medium size potatoes, cooked, peeled and diced**
- **1 bunch Swiss chard, washed, chopped and briefly steamed**
- **½ onion, chopped**
- **1 tomato, chopped**

1. Peel *chorizo* and crumble into skillet. Sauté 15 to 20 minutes. Drain all but 2 tablespoons of fat from pan.

Poultry and eggs

Since ancient times, wild and domestic fowl have been a succulent part of the Mexican menu.
Mexico gave the turkey to the world and happily adopted some of the native birds of Europe and Asia to fit into its own cuisine.

In the early Spanish chronicles of New Spain, numerous different birds are mentioned as part of the diet of the Aztecs. There were turkeys, quail, pigeons and many kinds of ducks and waterbirds. The turkey was domesticated, and some scholars believe that certain ducks were also.

Fowl was generally cooked by the Aztecs in covered underground pits, with a pot positioned over the hot stones to catch the drippings. The meat was covered with *mixiote,* a thin membrane from the leaf of the maguey plant. In spirit and technique, these earliest Mexican feasts are closely related to contemporary cuisine. *Moles,* in particular, are direct descendants of Aztec recipes.

Mole Poblano
(Chile sauce of Puebla)

There are many *moles* descended from the *chilmolli* of the Aztecs, but the richest are those served with *guajolote* (the Aztec word for turkey). Of these, *mole poblano* is probably the most famous. It does not use the fresh chile called *poblano,* but like the chile, its name comes from the city of Puebla. A cookbook published there in 1877 gave recipes for 44 different *moles.*

The story of the creation of *mole poblano* is told in many versions and probably reports a real event that occurred some 200 years ago. The sisters of Puebla's Convent of Santa Rosa, in honor of the visiting Viceroy, devised a *mole* of unusual (and possibly desperate) complexity, a brave

◁

Huevos Rancheros, a meal for breakfast, lunch or dinner. (Recipe on page 66.) The ceramic rooster at the top of this page is by Candelario Medrano Lopez.

combination of chiles, nuts, tomatoes, garlic, seeds, cinnamon, chocolate, etc. Whether through divine inspiration or devilish necessity, it was a success.

Just how close our recipe is to the original is hard to say. It is, however, devilishly good.

Mole Poblano para Guajolote o Pollo
(*Mole* for chicken or turkey)

- ⅔ cup whole almonds
- 6 dried *mulato* chiles
- 4 dried *ancho* chiles
- 4 dried *pasilla* chiles
  Water to cover
- ½ cup lard
- 8 pounds turkey or chicken, cut into serving size pieces
  Giblets
- 4 cups water
- 1 teaspoon salt
- ⅓ cup sesame seeds
- ¼ teaspoon anise seeds
- 1 cinnamon stick
- 4 cloves garlic, unpeeled
- ¼ cup lard
- 1 stale corn *tortilla*
- ¼ cup raisins
- ¼ teaspoon ground coriander seed
- ¼ teaspoon ground cloves
- 3 tablespoons lard
- ½ Mexican chocolate tablet
- 3½ cups reserved chicken or turkey broth

1. Toast the almonds in a 300 degree oven for 30 minutes. Set aside to cool.

2. Wash the chiles and warm them on a griddle over medium heat until soft. Remove the stems and all seeds. Open the chiles flat and place into a saucepan. Weigh them down with a plate and cover with water. Bring to a boil and allow to cook 5 minutes over medium heat. Set aside.

3. In a large skillet, heat ½ cup lard and brown the turkey or chicken pieces, 10 minutes on each side. Transfer to a baking dish and bake in

a 325 degree oven for 50 minutes for turkey, 30 minutes for chicken. Set aside.

4. In a saucepan, cover the giblets with 4 cups water and 1 teaspoon salt. Bring to a boil and simmer for 30 minutes. Drain and reserve the broth.

5. In an ungreased skillet, toast the sesame seeds over medium heat, tossing frequently, until golden. Remove from pan, reserve 2 tablespoons toasted sesame seeds and set aside. In the skillet, toast anise seeds, cinnamon stick and garlic over medium heat. Peel the garlic and set aside. In a blender, finely grind the cinnamon stick, anise and remainder of sesame seeds. Set aside.

6. Fry the stale corn *tortilla* in ¼ cup hot lard until crisp and golden. (If *tortilla* is not stale, dry slowly in 200 degree oven.) Fry the raisins, only briefly, to puff. Break *tortilla* in pieces into the blender. Blend into fine crumbs. Add the cooled, toasted almonds and blend until fine. Remove the mixture from the blender and set aside.

7. Place in the blender the garlic, raisins, cinnamon, anise and sesame mixture. Also add ¼ teaspoon *each* ground coriander and ground cloves. Drain the cooled chiles, reserving liquid. Add to the blender 1 cup chile liquid and the chiles. Blend briefly for an even consistency. Add the almond-*tortilla* mixture and ½ cup reserved turkey or chicken broth. Blend.

8. In a large pot, melt 3 tablespoons lard. Add the chile mixture and fry 5 minutes, stirring constantly. Break the chocolate into pieces and add to the chile purée, lower the heat and cook 10 minutes to melt the chocolate, stirring constantly. Slowly stir in the 3 cups reserved turkey or chicken

broth, bring to a boil, then lower heat and simmer for 30 minutes.

9. Add turkey or chicken pieces to *mole* and cook to heat through. Transfer to a serving dish and top with the reserved sesame seeds. Or place the turkey or chicken pieces in a bakeproof serving dish; pour *mole* over all. Cover and place in a 350 degree oven to heat through (approximately 20 minutes), remove cover, sprinkle with the reserved sesame seeds and serve. Serves 10 to 12.

Note: *Mole poblano* may be made in advance. Use the sauce within 2 days or freeze.

Shortcut Mole

Prepare the turkey or chicken as described above.

> 2 jars (8 oz. each) prepared *mole poblano* paste
> 5 to 6 cups turkey or chicken broth

Pour the oil that has separated from the mixture in the jars into a large pot. Heat the oil, add the *mole* paste from the jars and briefly fry over medium heat (3 minutes), stirring constantly. Slowly add the broth, continue stirring. Bring to a boil, immediately reduce to simmer. Add chicken or turkey pieces. See serving information above. Serves 8 to 10.

Mole Verde de Pepitas I
(Green pumpkin seed *mole*)

> 1 cup *pepitas* (hulled, unsalted pumpkin seeds)
> 6 *poblano* chiles, roasted, peeled and cleaned
> 2 cloves garlic, chopped
> ½ onion, chopped
> 2 cans (12 oz. each) *tomatillos*, drained
> ½ cup cilantro leaves
> 2 tablespoons lard
> 2 cups chicken broth
> Salt and pepper to taste
> 4 pounds precooked chicken, duck or pork

1. In an ungreased skillet, toast the *pepitas* over medium-low heat until all have puffed. Allow the *pepitas* to cool. Grind fine in the blender. Remove the *pepitas* from the blender and set aside.

2. Place in the blender the prepared chiles, garlic, onion, *tomatillos* and cilantro. Blend smooth. Add the *pepitas* and again blend until smooth.

3. Heat the lard and fry the prepared purée for 3 minutes over medium heat, stirring constantly. Slowly add the chicken broth, stirring until smooth. Add salt and pepper to taste. Reduce heat and simmer 15 minutes.

◊

The turkey for mole poblano *is cooked very simply, but the sauce requires quite a few ingredients, including three kinds of chiles and chocolate.*

4. Add the precooked meat to heat through. Never allow to boil.

Keeps well up to 3 days. Reheat in double boiler. Serves 6 to 8.

Mole Verde de Pepitas II

> 2 pounds chicken, veal or pork chopped
> ½ teaspoon salt
> 1 pound *tomatillos*
> 2 or 3 *serrano* chiles
> 4 ounces hulled pumpkin seeds
> 1 small onion
> 2 sprigs fresh cilantro
> 1 lettuce or romaine leaf
> 1 avocado leaf (if available)
> 2 tablespoons lard or oil
> Salt and pepper to taste

1. Cook the meat in a small amount of water with ½ teaspoon salt, until tender.

2. Remove the husks of the *tomatillos* and the stems of the chiles. Discard chile seeds also, if a milder sauce is desired, or substitute fresh or canned green chiles.

3. Blend all the ingredients except the meat and oil in an electric blender. Heat the oil and sauté the blended mixture, stirring constantly, until it thickens to the desired consistency.

4. Add the meat. Simmer only long enough to allow the meat to absorb the taste of the sauce. Season to taste. Serve hot over rice. Serves 4 to 6.

Mole Verde con Nueces
(Green *mole* sauce with nuts)

> 2 ounces almonds, blanched
> 2 ounces walnuts
> 2 ounces peanuts
> 4 tablespoons oil
> ¾ pound large, mild green chiles, coarsely chopped
> 1 tablespoon flour
> 2 cups chicken stock
> Salt and pepper

1. Roast the almonds, walnuts and peanuts in half the oil.

2. Wash the chiles in cold water and discard the stems.

3. In a blender, blend the toasted nuts and chiles, using as little water as necessary.

4. In a skillet toast the flour in the rest of the oil. Add the blended mixture and the chicken broth and simmer 1 hour. Season with salt and pepper.

This sauce is particularly good with precooked chicken or turkey. Serves 6 to 8.

Pipianes

Pipianes are a *mole* of a different color. Less complicated than the *mole poblano,* they do not use the green chiles and *tomatillos* of *mole verde.*

Pipián de Almendras
(Almond *pipián*)

> 6 dried *ancho* chiles
> ½ cup unblanched almonds or 1 cup either pumpkin seeds or sesame seeds
> 2 tablespoons lard or oil
> 2 cups chicken stock
> ⅛ teaspoon ground cloves
> ⅛ teaspoon cinnamon
> Salt and pepper

1. Rinse the chiles in cold water. Discard the stems but reserve the seeds until later. Soak the chiles for at least one hour in just enough hot water to cover.

2. Toast the almonds and chile seeds but do not allow them to burn. Then grind the almonds, chile seeds and chiles as fine as possible.

3. Sauté the ground ingredients in the lard or oil. Add the chicken stock and simmer until it begins to thicken. Add the spices and season with salt and pepper.

The feet come with the fowl — they are valued particularly for making broth.

4. To the *pipián* sauce add pre-cooked chicken, turkey, tongue or other meats. Simmer in the sauce only long enough for them to absorb the seasoning. Serves 6 to 8.

Pipián Rápido
(Quick *pipián*)
The recipe below makes use of a canned sauce. Don't be surprised that it contains peanut butter. Many Mexican sauces employ peanuts, pumpkin seeds, sesame seeds, or almonds as thickening agents and for flavor. Your guests probably will be unable to guess the source of the delicious taste.

- **1 large can (27 oz.) red chile sauce**
- **1½ tablespoons creamy peanut butter**
- **¼ teaspoon oregano**
- **½ teaspoon salt**

Heat the sauce in a large skillet. Add the peanut butter and simmer until the peanut butter has blended with the chile. Add oregano and salt.

This sauce is excellent with pre-cooked chicken, turkey, pork, tongue, or other meats. Add the meat to the sauce and simmer together for a few minutes to allow the sauce to season the meat. The whole dish may be prepared days in advance of need and frozen. Serve with a Mexican rice or pasta. Serves 6 to 8.

Pollo Almendrado
(Almond chicken)

- **¾ cup whole almonds, blanched**
- **3 pounds chicken pieces (cut-up whole chicken or chicken breasts)**
  Lard for frying, ½ inch deep
- **½ cup crushed pineapple**
- **1 cup fresh, seedless grapes (or 1 small can (8-oz.) whole grapes, drained)**
- **1 cup orange juice**
- **1 cup dry white wine**
- **2 tablespoons honey (only if using fresh grapes)**
- **¼ teaspoon cinnamon**
- **⅛ teaspoon cloves**
- **⅛ teaspoon thyme**

1. Toast the almonds in a 300 degree oven for 30 minutes. Set aside to cool.

2. Grind ½ cup of almonds in blender or *molcajete* until fine. Chop ¼ cup coarsely.

3. Brown the chicken pieces in the hot oil (370 degrees), 10 minutes on each side. Place chicken in single layer in a shallow glass baking pan.

4. Combine all other ingredients, including almonds, and pour over chicken.

5. Bake at 325 degrees for 40 minutes. Baste several times. Increase temperature to 350 degrees and bake an additional 10 minutes. May be

garnished with slivers of orange peel. Serves 4.

Pollo con Salsa de Cacahuate
(Chicken with peanut sauce)

- **2 pounds chicken, cut up**
- **½ teaspoon salt**
- **1 pound tomatoes, peeled**
- **6 ounces peanuts**
- **½ small French roll or 1 slice white bread, browned in oil**
- **1 small onion, chopped**
- **1 garlic clove**
- **4 cloves**
- **2 tablespoons lard or oil**
  Salt and pepper to taste

1. Half cover the chicken with salted water, cover and cook until tender.

2. Blend remaining ingredients except lard in an electric blender. Heat the lard or oil and sauté sauce, adding a little of the cooking liquid. Stir until thick. Season to taste.

3. Add the chicken and simmer only long enough for it to absorb the taste. Serves 4 to 6. (Pork or veal may be substituted.)

Relleno para Guajolote
(Turkey stuffing)
This recipe was given to us by a Texas-born friend, Carmen Salazar Parr, who inherited it from her mother. It is not sweet but it is a bit spicy.

- **Turkey giblets and neck**
- **1 pound lean pork, cut into several pieces**
- **½ teaspoon salt**
- **1½ cups celery, finely chopped**
- **½ cup onion, finely chopped**
- **3 tablespoons margarine or butter**
- **¼ pound mild ham, chopped**
- **¼ teaspoon ground cumin**
- **¼ teaspoon ground thyme**
- **2 small loaves French bread (not sourdough), minus end crusts**
- **1 cup dry white wine**
- **8 to 12 ripe olives, chopped**
- **½ to 1 cup seedless raisins, plumped in warm water, or dry prunes, chopped**
- **½ cup walnuts or pecans, finely chopped**
- **1 teaspoon salt**
- **¼ teaspoon pepper**

1. Cover giblets, neck and pork with water and simmer until tender. Add ½ teaspoon salt during first 15 minutes. Cool enough to handle and chop fine or grind.

2. Sauté celery and onion in the margarine or butter until the celery is partially done. Add chopped ham and other meats, cumin, and thyme, and cook together for a few minutes.

3. Cube bread and dry in oven but do not brown. Sprinkle wine over bread and mix well.

4. Add the olives, raisins, nuts, salt and pepper and mix all ingredients well. Use some of the giblet broth for additional moistening, if needed.

Makes enough stuffing for medium-size turkey.

Huevos

Egg dishes are also very important in Mexico and are often prepared as a main dish. Turkeys and chickens are too expensive for everyday fare for most people and are often saved for celebrations. But the eggs that are laid must be eaten, and, since chickens are kept by many city people as well as country people, eggs are a big part of the animal protein in the Mexican diet.

Huevos Rancheros
(Country-style eggs)
This is a hardy breakfast or brunch dish, perhaps the best known of all Mexican egg dishes.

- **6 corn *tortillas***
- **6 eggs**
- **3 tablespoons lard or oil**

1. Fry the *tortillas* on both sides until lightly browned but not crisp. Drain on absorbent paper.

2. Top each *tortilla* with a fried egg.

3. Spoon hot *Salsa frita* (recipe follows) over the eggs.

(As an alternate, poach the eggs in the *salsa* and spoon the unbroken eggs and *salsa* on to the fried *tortillas* and serve.)

Salsa Frita

- **2 large tomatoes, peeled and finely chopped**
- **1 small onion, finely chopped**
- **1 clove garlic, minced or mashed**
- **2 or 3 canned mild green chiles, chopped (or for much hotter sauce, substitute 1 or more fresh or canned *serrano* or *jalapeño* chiles, rinsed in cold water, seeded, and chopped)**
- **1 teaspoon salt**
- **2 tablespoons lard or oil**

Mix all the ingredients except lard. Sauté in hot lard for about 5 minutes over low heat. Serve hot. A couple of sprigs of chopped fresh cilantro or some crumbled dry oregano can be added just before serving. Serves 6.

Huevos con Chorizo
(Eggs with sausage)

- **1 pound *chorizo* (Mexican sausage), at least ¼ pound per serving**
- **½ cup onion, chopped**
- **1 tomato, chopped**
- **¼ cup cilantro leaves, slightly chopped**
- **8 eggs, slightly beaten (4 eggs for a spicier mixture)**

1. Peel chorizo and crumble into skillet. Sauté 15 to 20 minutes. Drain excess fat.

2. Add onion and tomato, cook until soft.

3. Add cilantro, eggs, and continue to cook until set to individual taste. Serves 4.

Shoppers bring their own egg baskets to Mexican markets — this bright colored basket is made from anodized aluminum.

Huevos con Sesos
(Egg with brains)

2 pair calf's brains
1 quart cold water
1½ tablespoons vinegar
2 cups water
½ teaspoon salt
4 tablespoons butter
½ onion, chopped
**1 fresh *serrano, jalapeño* or *güero*
  chile, washed, seeded and finely
  chopped**
1 large tomato, chopped
6 to 8 eggs
  **Sprig of *epazote* or 2 tablespoons
  cilantro leaves, slightly chopped**
  Salt and pepper to taste

1. Rinse the brains in cold water. Soak for 1 hour in 1 quart cold water with 1 tablespoon of the vinegar added.

2. Carefully pull away the membrane and trim. Rinse again in cold water.

3. Bring to a boil 2 cups water, ½ teaspoon salt, ½ tablespoon vinegar. Reduce heat to simmer and add the brains. Cook for 30 minutes, drain, rinse, cool and chop.

4. In a skillet, melt the butter and sauté the onion until soft. Add the chopped chiles and tomato; cook briefly until the tomato is soft. Add the brains and sauté to heat through.

5. Whip the eggs, add them to the skillet with the *epazote* or cilantro and cook until set. Salt and pepper to taste. Serves 4.

Huevos Revueltos
(Mexican style scrambled eggs)

In our house this is a common Sunday morning breakfast or, with the addition of refried beans and hot *tortillas,* an excellent brunch.

**1 large tomato, peeled, seeded and
  chopped**
3 tablespoons minced onion
**3 canned mild green chiles, or fresh,
  seeded and chopped**
3 tablespoons butter
6 eggs, lightly beaten
  Salt and pepper to taste

1. Sauté the tomato, onion, and chiles in butter until the onion is soft.

2. Add the seasoned, beaten eggs and scramble.

3. Serve with hot *tortillas.* Serves 3.

Huevos con Flor de Calabaza
(Eggs with squash blossoms)

1 pound squash or pumpkin blossoms
3 tablespoons butter
½ small onion, chopped
  Sprig of *epazote*
1 tomato, chopped
8 eggs
  **Queso fresco (cheese), crumbled
  (optional)**

1. Wash and chop the blossoms.

2. In a skillet, heat the butter and gently sauté the blossoms, onions and *epazote;* when soft, add the tomato and allow it to soften. Remove the *epazote.*

3. Whip the eggs and add to the skillet, cooking until set.

4. Each serving may be topped with a sprinkle of the crumbled cheese. Serves 4 to 6.

Huevos con Nopales
(Eggs with cactus)

3 tablespoons butter
½ onion, finely chopped
1 tomato, chopped
**1 cup cooked *nopales* (cactus leaves)
  or 1 small jar, drained and
  chopped**
8 eggs
  Few sprigs cilantro leaves
  **Queso fresco (cheese), crumbled
  (optional)**

1. In a skillet, heat the butter and sauté the onion, tomato and cactus; cook until the onion is soft.

2. Whip the eggs and add to the skillet, cooking until set.

3. Stir in cilantro and serve. Top each serving with an optional sprinkling of crumbled *queso fresco.* Serves 4.

Fish and shellfish

A drive across the width of Mexico is enough to convince you that all Mexicans, coastal and interior, are seafood addicts. The variety of seafood offered is probably equaled only in the Orient.

Since Mexicans are by and large seafood fanatics, scrupulously fresh seafood is offered in markets across the country. Wherever transportation allows rapid delivery, there are open-front cafes serving nothing but *pescados* and *mariscos*. (Seafood cocktails and entrées in coastal restaurants are so good that, to us, other choices seem silly.) This seafood habit is of ancient lineage. The Emperor Montezuma ordered fresh fish brought from the Gulf by relays of runners all the way to his palace in what is now Mexico City.

With good, fresh fish and shellfish, the simplest cooking methods are generally the best — charcoal grilling, frying or baking.

Mexico is long on seacoast and short on rivers and streams. The fish served in inland Mexico usually comes from the ocean, though some regions do produce remarkably good fresh-water fish.

Each village and city along the Mexican coast has its own prized recipes. It would be impossible to catalog all of them here, but we are pleased to be able to present the predominant styles and techniques.

Huachinango a la Veracruzana
(Red snapper Vera Cruz style)
This has been our favorite and most popular fish recipe. The slightly exotic odors and taste of the spices and the bite of the *jalapeños* make it a dish for even those who "don't like fish."

We particularly like it for its convenience. We prepare the sauce in large quantities and find that it freezes beautifully. The sauce can be

◁

On the beach at Puerto Vallarta, Señor Ramon Gutiérrez broils whole fish slowly over charcoal fire.

used equally well for *any* mild firm-fleshed fish.

- 1 large onion, chopped
- 3 cloves garlic, minced
- ¼ cup olive oil
- 8 tomatoes, peeled, seeded and chopped
- 3 canned *jalapeño* chiles, drained, seeded and cut into narrow strips
- 1 small jar pitted green olives, plain or pimiento-stuffed, drained
- ¼ teaspoon cinnamon
- ¼ teaspoon ground cloves
- ½ teaspoon sugar
- Juice of ½ lemon
- 1 teaspoon salt
- 1 tablespoon capers (optional)
- 3 pounds red snapper fillets
- Flour seasoned with salt and pepper
- 1 tablespoon fresh chopped parsley or cilantro (as garnish)

1. Sauté the onions and garlic in a little of the olive oil, but do not brown. Add the tomatoes, chiles, olives, cinnamon, cloves, sugar, lemon juice and salt. Simmer on a low heat for about five minutes. Add capers if desired. Cover and set aside until the fish is cooked.

2. Dust the fish fillets lightly with the seasoned flour and sauté in oil until golden brown on both sides and easily flaked with a fork.

3. Arrange the fish on a heated platter. Spoon the sauce over the fish. Garnish with the chopped parsley or cilantro. Serves 6.

Huachinango con Jugo de Naranja
(Red snapper with orange juice)

- 2 pounds red snapper fillets
- ½ cup minced onion
- 2 cloves garlic, minced
- ½ cup parsley, chopped
- ¼ cup oil
- 2 cups orange juice
- 2 tablespoons butter
- 15 to 20 pitted green olives, halved
- 3 (or more) canned pickled *jalapeño* chiles, seeded and chopped
- Salt and pepper to taste

1. Arrange red snapper fillets in a lightly buttered baking dish. Score each fillet with a sharp knife.

2. In a skillet, sauté onions, garlic, and parsley in the oil until tender but not browned. Add orange juice and mix. Season to taste.

3. Dot fish with butter. Arrange olives and chiles evenly over the fillets. Pour the sauce over the fish. Bake at 350 degrees for 25 to 30 minutes. Serve hot. Serves 4 to 6.

Huachinango Almendrado
(Red snapper with almonds)

- 1 or 2 whole red snappers (about 2 pounds), scaled and cleaned, or 1½ pounds filleted fish
- ½ cup cilantro or parsley, chopped (or combination)
- ½ cup almonds, toasted and finely chopped
- 4 tablespoons butter
- Juice of 2 limes
- ½ teaspoon salt
- ¼ teaspoon pepper

Curious to see the catch, onlookers wait while the fishermen pull in their nets along the seawall beach at Vera Cruz.

For Camarones Escorpionados en Chile Rojo, *shrimp are cut along underside rather than the back, causing them to curl differently when they are cooked.*

1. Score the fish by making diagonal cuts along the sides. Place the fish in a baking pan.

2. Sprinkle the chopped cilantro or parsley and chopped almonds over the fish.

3. Melt butter; add lime juice, salt and pepper, and pour over the fish.

4. Cover the pan with foil and bake in a moderate oven until just tender, approximately 30 minutes. Serves 4.

Seviche
(Marinated raw fish)

1 pound firm, white, ocean fish (scallops, turbot, etc.) in small cubes
  Lime or lemon juice
½ small onion, in thin rounds, separated into rings
1 small firm tomato, peeled, seeded, and diced
  Chiles (2 or 3 canned *serrano* or *jalapeño* chiles, seeded and chopped)
3 tablespoons oil
2 tablespoons vinegar
  Salt to taste
  Fresh chopped cilantro or ½ teaspoon dried oregano

1. In a glass or porcelain bowl, cover

the fish with lime or lemon juice. Marinate for more than 4 hours or overnight in the refrigerator. Turn once or twice to be sure that all surfaces are "cooked" by the citrus juice.

2. Add remaining ingredients and mix gently. Serve chilled. Serves 4 to 6.

Seviche de Jaiba y Camarones
(Crab and shrimp *seviche*)
This is an attractive and delicious salad or cocktail for a special occasion. The color combinations make it especially appealing.

8 ounces shrimp, fresh or frozen, cleaned
½ cup lime or lemon juice
8 ounces crabmeat, fresh or frozen, flaked
2 tablespoons onion, finely chopped
1 small tomato, seeded and chopped
1 tablespoon cilantro, chopped
2 canned pickled *jalapeño* chiles, seeded and chopped
  Salt and pepper to taste
1 avocado, peeled and sliced
6 stuffed green olives, sliced

1. In a glass bowl marinate the shrimp overnight in the citrus juice.

2. In the morning, add the crabmeat and all the ingredients except the avocado and olives. Mix and chill for another 2 hours.

3. Divide among 6 cocktail glasses or arrange on a lettuce leaf on small salad plates. Garnish with avocado and olive slices. Serves 4 to 6.

Pescado en Escabeche
(Fish in vinegar)

2 pounds mild, firm-fleshed fish, sliced
½ cup oil
1 onion, thinly sliced
2 cloves garlic, minced
3 large, mild, green chiles, roasted, peeled, cleaned and chopped (or 3 canned green chiles, coarsely chopped)
20 ripe olives
½ cup (or more) vinegar
2 limes in ¼ inch slices, or
3 tablespoons lime juice
1 teaspoon salt
  Pepper to taste

1. Sauté the fish slices in oil until golden brown on both sides. Arrange in a glass serving dish with cover.

2. Mix the remaining oil in which the fish was fried and the other ingredi-

ents. Pour over fish. If necessary, add more vinegar to cover the fish completely.

3. Refrigerate 2 to 4 days before serving. Serves 6 to 8.

Camarones Escorpionados en Chile Rojo
(Scorpion-cut shrimp in red chile)

1½ pounds medium size shrimp, shelled but with tails left on, deveined

Open the shrimp by cutting with a sharp knife down the length of the shrimp on the underside to form a hinge. (When cooked they resemble a striking scorpion.) Cook the shrimp in boiling, salted water just until they turn pink. Drain.

Sauce

**3 dried *ancho* chiles
2 dried *pasilla* chiles
3 large whole tomatoes
3 cloves garlic, chopped
1 teaspoon salt
¼ teaspoon oregano
3 green onions, finely chopped**

1. On the *comal* or griddle, over medium-low heat, cook the chiles, only to soften. Remove the stems and most of the seeds. Open the chiles flat and place in a saucepan, weighted down with a plate. Barely cover the chiles with water, bring to a boil and cook for 5 minutes over medium heat. Set aside at least for ½ hour.

2. Broil the tomatoes, about 15 minutes, turning several times, until soft and cooked through.

3. Drain the chiles and place in the blender with the garlic, tomatoes, salt and oregano. Blend briefly for an even consistency. Stir in the chopped onion.

4. Serve the sauce and shrimp separately. The sauce may be either hot or chilled.

As a main course the shrimp may be added to the heated sauce and served on a bed of white rice. Accompany this meal with avocado and melon wedges. This sauce will keep only 2 days refrigerated; however, it freezes well. Serves 6 as a first course.

Camarones al Mojo de Ajo
(Broiled garlic shrimp)

**1 pound medium-size shrimp
5 tablespoons butter
2 or 3 large cloves garlic, minced or mashed
⅛ teaspoon mild powdered chile (optional)
1 tablespoon lime or lemon juice**

1. Peel shrimp, leaving the tail for a handle. Remove vein.

2. Melt butter in a small pan. Add garlic, powdered chile and lime or lemon juice. Simmer 1 minute.

3. Place shrimp on skewers (double-prong type keeps shrimp flat).

4. Baste with butter mixture and broil over hot coals, turning once, just until pink — about 3 minutes. Be careful not to overcook the shrimp as they will toughen. Serves 6 to 8 as an appetizer.

Camarones en Escabeche
(Pickled shrimp)

**1 pound fresh shrimp, cleaned and peeled
Flour
Salt and pepper
⅓ cup oil
2 bay leaves
½ teaspoon powdered cumin
½ teaspoon ground nutmeg
2 cloves garlic, mashed
1 tablespoon paprika
1 cup vinegar
1 small onion, thinly sliced
2 or 3 canned *jalapeño* chiles, cut in strips
Salt and pepper to taste
Lettuce or romaine leaves
Radishes, sliced
Green olives, sliced**

1. Toss the shrimp in seasoned flour.

2. Sauté a few at a time in a little oil until lightly brown, adding oil as needed.

3. Place in a covered serving dish.

4. Combine any oil remaining from the frying in a saucepan with the bay leaves, cumin, nutmeg, garlic, paprika, vinegar, onion, chiles, and salt and pepper to taste. Bring to a boil slowly and simmer until onion is tender. Pour sauce over shrimp. Cool, then chill overnight.

5. Serve cold on lettuce or romaine leaves, garnished with slices of radish and green olives. Serves 4 to 6.

Jaibas Rellenas de Tampico
(Stuffed crabs Tampico style)
This recipe was sent to us from Tampico by Gwen Dunning.

**½ cup onion, finely chopped
1 clove garlic, minced
1 pound tomatoes, blanched, peeled, and chopped
½ teaspoon sugar
12 pimiento-stuffed ripe olives, chopped
2 tablespoons fresh parsley, minced
10 ounces crab meat, cooked and shredded
¼ cup white wine
Salt and pepper to taste
Bread crumbs, soft and fresh
2 tablespoons butter
12 small crab shells (optional)**

1. Fry the onion and garlic in a small amount of oil until the onion is transparent. Add the tomatoes, sugar, olives and parsley. Simmer gently until the mixture begins to thicken.

2. Add the crab meat, wine, and salt and pepper to taste. Divide among 12 small, clean crab shells or

6 individual casseroles. Sprinkle each with bread crumbs and top with bits of butter.

3. Bake at 350 degrees for 15 minutes or until brown. Serves 6.

Arroz con Jaibas
(Rice with crab)

**¼ cup lard or oil
2 tablespoons *achiote* seeds
2 cups long grain rice
1 small onion, chopped
2 cloves garlic, crushed
3 tomatoes, thin wedged and halved
3 *poblano* or 4 Anaheim chiles, roasted, peeled, cleaned and torn into strips
3 cups chicken stock
1 cup dry white wine
1 to 1½ pounds crab meat
Salt and freshly ground pepper to taste, if necessary**

Early morning catch is rinsed and sorted at the beach.

Three lovely pink Pacific snappers come to the kitchen ready to scale.

Covered with cilantro and almonds the snappers are ready for the oven. (Page 69.)

1. In a large skillet or pot, preheat the lard or oil and fry the *achiote* seeds over low heat. When the oil is deep orange and the seeds dark, remove and discard the *achiote*.

2. Add the rice and fry over medium heat until puffed and all oil is absorbed. Add the onion and garlic and cook until soft. Add the tomatoes and chile strips; cook until the tomato is soft.

3. Pour in the chicken stock and wine, bring to a boil, cover and cook over medium heat for 20 minutes.

4. Lay the crab meat on top of the rice mixture. Cover and simmer for an additional 20 minutes until all liquid has been absorbed.

5. Thoroughly toss the rice to mix the crab throughout. Serves 8.

Ensalada de Camarones
(Shrimp salad)

This recipe calls for mayonnaise, often believed to be a French inven-tion but probably it is Spanish, and is called *salsa mahonesa,* after the city of Mahon on the island of Minorca. It may have come to Mexico with the Spanish but more likely with the French occupation during the nineteenth century.

France apparently took the garlic out of the original Spanish mayon-naise; you'll note that Mexico has put the garlic back, at least for this recipe.

---

  2 pounds shrimp, peeled
  ¾ cup mayonnaise
  3 large, mild green chiles, roasted, peeled, cleaned and chopped (or 1 small can green chiles, seeded and chopped)
  1 small clove garlic, minced
  2 tablespoons onion, minced
     Lettuce or romaine leaves
  1 canned *jalapeño* chile, seeded and chopped (optional for hotter taste)

---

1. Cook shrimp in boiling salted water until they turn pink. Drain. Rinse with cold water to cool. Devein.

2. Cut into bite-size pieces unless shrimp are very small. Combine with other ingredients.

3. Serve on lettuce leaves. Serves 6.

Tortas de Camarón con Nopales
(Shrimp patties with cactus)

This traditional Lenten dish from Doña Maria Garcia Quintero has been modified to allow the use of fresh shrimp.

---

  4 cups diced fresh *nopales* or 2 jars (16 oz. each) diced cactus
  2 large, mild, green chiles, roasted, peeled, cleaned and cut in strips
  4 dried *ancho* chiles
  ½ teaspoon salt
  2 large tomatoes (about 1¼ pounds)
  1 small onion, chopped
  ½ teaspoon oregano
  ¼ teaspoon peppercorns
  1 clove garlic
  ½ teaspoon salt
  1 teaspoon sugar
  1 tablespoon oil

---

1. If using fresh *nopales,* clean away any spines with a sharp knife. Trim and wash cactus and cut into ½ inch pieces. Cover with water, add ½ teaspoon salt, cook until tender. (Usually 20 to 30 minutes, depending on the thickness.) Drain in a colander and cover with a damp, wrung-out towel. Set aside. If using canned cactus, rinse well and drain.

2. Roast, peel and clean the chiles. Cut them into strips.

3. Toast the dried chiles, only to soften. Remove seeds and veins.

4. Half cover the tomatoes and dried chiles with water and cook until soft.

5. Put the tomatoes, *ancho* chiles, onion, oregano, peppercorns, garlic, salt and sugar in the blender. Blend, using enough of the cooking water to have 4 cups. Strain.

6. Heat oil. Fry green chile strips and *nopales* until soft. Add the blender mixture and simmer for 30 minutes.

Patties

---

  4 eggs, separated
  4 to 5 ounces cooked shrimp, finely chopped (or 2 oz. dried powdered shrimp, lightly toasted)
  ⅔ cup cooked beans, mashed well
  1 tablespoon flour
     Salt and pepper to taste
     Oil for frying, ½ inch deep

---

1. Beat egg whites until stiff.

2. Lightly beat egg yolks, add shrimp, beans, flour, and salt and pepper. Fold into egg whites. the egg whites.

3. Spoon enough of the egg mixture to make 2½ - to 3-inch patties into ½ inch hot (375 degrees) oil. Fry on both sides until golden brown.

4. Drain on paper towel. Serve hot in the cactus sauce. Salt and pepper to taste. Serves 6.

Our seviche *shown here was made with scallops. In Mexico, sierra and corvina are most often used, but most firm, white, ocean fish are suitable. (See page 70.)*

(If necessary, the patties may be made early, then reheated briefly in a hot oven.)

Ensalada de Queso Asadero
(*Asadero* cheese salad)

Shredded iceberg lettuce
Oil and vinegar dressing, page 77
½ cup precooked, chilled shrimp, crab or flaked red snapper
2 slices *Asadero* cheese (good substitutions are large, round, thin slices of provolone or mozarella cheese)
Guacamole, page 76
Lime or lemon wedges

1. For each serving, line plate with shredded lettuce. Sprinkle oil and vinegar dressing over the lettuce.

2. Place ½ cup fish or shellfish in the center of each cheese slice.

3. Roll and place on the bed of lettuce.

4. Top with *guacamole.* Garnish with a wedge of lime or lemon. Serves 1.

Traditional shrimp tortas *prepared by Doña Maria Garcia Quintero are made from dried whole shrimp and combined with sauce immediately before serving.*

Abulón
(Abalone)

Native to the Pacific Coast, the abalone is a shellfish well known to gourmets and scuba divers from San Francisco to the southern coasts of Mexico. It is particularly plentiful along the coasts of Baja California, where an overabundance of skindivers has not yet depleted the supply. On the west coast it can be bought either fresh or frozen. In its frozen state, it is now being distributed to other parts of the country.

The most common way to prepare this very delicate tasting shellfish is to slice it into ⅜ inch slices, pound it until it is tender, then sauté, either plain, floured or breaded, in butter or parsley butter. Fry for one minute *only* each side. It will toughen if cooked longer.

Canned abalone is sold in Mexican markets and can be bought in stores which handle Mexican imports. Canned abalone lends itself to use in seafood cocktails, as an appetizer, either in sauce or pickled.

This recipe comes from a friend deep in the heart of Mexico even though it includes ingredients like Worcestershire sauce and catsup. Both of these are now produced in Mexico and are common items on Mexican tables. It is natural that they appear in modern recipes.

Coctel de Abulón
(Abalone cocktail)

1 can (1 lb.) abalone, cut into small cubes
2 tablespoons Worcestershire sauce (*salsa inglesa* in Spanish)
¼ cup white wine
Juice of 2 limes or lemons
1 canned pickled *jalapeño* chile, seeded and minced
2 sprigs parsley, chopped
Tomato catsup
Salt and pepper
2 avocados, peeled and sliced

Mix all the ingredients except the avocados with enough catsup to reach desired consistency. Season to taste. Chill. Serve in icers or cocktail glasses garnished with avocado slices. Serves 6 to 8.

Bocaditos de Abulón
(Abalone toothpick tidbits)

1 can (1 lb.) abalone, cubed
Juice of 2 lemons or limes
Fresh chile *salsa* (see recipe, page 26)

Mix cubed abalone with a small amount of its own juice and the juice of two lemons or limes, and season to taste. Chill. Serve on toothpicks with a fresh chile *salsa* made with *serrano* or *jalapeño* chiles. Serves 6.

Abulón en Escabeche
(Abalone in vinegar)

1 can (1 lb.) abalone, thinly sliced
Salt and pepper
Flour
Olive oil
⅔ cup vinegar
1 small onion, sliced
⅛ teaspoon ground cumin
1 bay leaf

1. Dredge the abalone lightly in seasoned flour.

2. Sauté in oil, *not more than one minute on each side.*

3. Place in a covered glass or porcelain container.

4. Strain any of the oil remaining from the frying of the abalone and mix it with vinegar, onion, cumin, and bay leaf. Heat to boiling and remove from heat. Pour over the abalone.

5. Cover the dish and refrigerate for several days. Serve as an appetizer, either chilled or at room temperature. Serves 6.

Vegetables and salads

Unembellished vegetables (verduras) raw or cooked are a rarity on the Mexican table, but vegetables are incorporated into almost every dish and meal, suitably enhanced, of course.

Vegetables are rarely taken "straight" in Mexican cooking. This doesn't mean that vegetables aren't important in meals; it just means that Mexican cooking leaves about as little place for raw, unadorned vegetables as Chinese cooking does. If a vegetable is cooked plain, you can be sure the fact will be hidden under a colorful sauce and a few garnishes.

Fresh vegetables such as zucchini, green peas, and fresh corn are often cooked with a batter as fritters. They are also cooked in *budines* — puddings made with flour, cheese, and eggs. Uncooked vegetables are served as *salsas* and garnishes on *antojitos*.

Dry beans are an exception to the above and are regularly cooked and served plain as *frijoles de olla*.

Quelites means greens, and covers a variety of plants used for cooked greens which are unfamiliar in most of the U.S. Many are collected as wild greens. The meaning of *quelites* seems to change in different areas of Mexico, probably dependent on the availability of specific wild greens. In the southwestern U.S.A., *quelites* is likely to mean lamb's quarters *(epazote)*. In other areas, it is used to designate purslane *(verdolagas)*. Most of the common greens used in the U.S. can be substituted, or you can grow your own purslane and lamb's quarters. (Get starter seeds from a neighbor or nursery.)

Mexican markets offer a wide selection of vegetables including just about anything you'll find in the U.S. as well as these unfamiliar ones.

◁

Chayotes *are picked from an overhead arbor near Orizaba, Vera Cruz.*

Chayote

The pale green *chayote,* which is a native of Mexico, is now becoming more available in markets in American metropolitan centers. It has been exported into Europe from North Africa for many years as a prized gourmet vegetable.

It can be mashed and served with butter, salt and pepper, served in cold salads, or even prepared as a dessert (page 88).

For more information see Ingredients, page 14, also Garden, page 19.

Chayotes con Elotes y Chile Verde
(Chayotes with corn and green chile)

1 small onion, finely chopped
2 ounces butter
2 ears fresh corn (cut kernels from cobs)
3 large mild green chiles, fresh or canned, seeded and cut into strips
3 *chayotes,* peeled and cubed
1 cup milk, or slightly more
**   Salt and pepper to taste**
3 ounces grated Parmesan or Romano cheese

1. In 1½ quart saucepan sauté onion in butter until soft but not browned.

2. Add the kernels of fresh corn and chiles; cook for another 5 minutes.

3. Add *chayotes* and milk. Mix gently. Season with salt and pepper. Cover and simmer gently until the *chayotes* and corn are tender.

4. Place in a serving bowl and sprinkle with grated cheese. Serve hot. Makes 6 servings.

Chayotes con Huevos
(Chayotes with eggs)

4 small *chayotes*
**   Butter or oil**
4 eggs
**   Salt and pepper**

1. Boil *chayotes* in salted water until just tender. Drain. Peel and dice.

2. Sauté in a little butter or oil.

3. Beat eggs. Add to *chayote* and scramble lightly. Add salt and pepper to taste. Serve immediately. Serves 4 to 6.

Mezcla de Verduras con Chiles
(Cabbage succotash)

4 cups sliced cabbage
2 tablespoons lard or oil
1 cup corn, cooked
2 *poblano* or Anaheim chiles, roasted, peeled and cleaned, cut in strips
1 tomato, chopped
**   Salt and pepper**

1. Sauté sliced cabbage in lard for 5 minutes.

2. Add corn, chile strips and tomato. Stir and cook until the cabbage is just tender. Add salt and pepper to taste. Serves 6.

Quelites
(Greens)

2 pounds *quelites* (mustard, spinach, lamb's quarters, dandelion greens)
1 small onion, chopped
1 clove garlic, minced
1 tablespoon oil
1 or 2 Anaheim chiles, roasted, peeled, cleaned and chopped
2 or 3 small tomatoes, chopped
**   Sour cream**

1. Cut off tough stalk ends of greens, wash and coarsely chop remaining leaves. Cook in large pot in small amount of boiling salted water until tender and drain. If using dandelion or other greens that may be bitter, drain and change cooking water one or two times.

2. In another pan, sauté onion and garlic in oil. Add chiles and then chopped tomatoes. Cook few minutes more.

3. Add mixture to cooked greens and serve with sour cream. Serves 4 to 6.

Chicharitos a la Mexicana
(Small green peas Mexican style)

    1 tablespoon lard or butter
    1 clove garlic
    ½ onion, chopped
    1 tomato, chopped
    1 package (10 oz.) frozen small
      green peas
    ¼ teaspoon salt
    2 tablespoons water

    1. Melt the lard, add the garlic clove and allow it to toast until golden. Remove the garlic and discard.

    2. Sauté onion over high heat until cooked soft. Add tomato and cook until soft.

    3. Place frozen peas in the skillet and add the salt and water. Stir and break up frozen block. Bring to a boil, reduce heat, cover and simmer for 10 minutes. Serves 4.

    Variation: Cut 1 pound fresh green beans into bite-size pieces, steam until fork tender. Set aside and proceed with above recipe.

Elote con Crema
(Corn and cream)

    3 tablespoons butter
    ½ onion, chopped
    1 clove garlic, crushed
    2 poblano chiles, roasted, peeled,
      cleaned and torn into strips (rajas)
    1 tomato, chopped
    1 package (10 oz.) frozen corn
    ½ teaspoon salt
    ¼ teaspoon pepper
    ½ cup half-and-half
    ½ pound cream cheese, cut into
      small pieces

    1. In a skillet, melt the butter and sauté the onion and garlic until the onion is soft.

    2. Add the chile rajas, then the tomato. Cook a minute to soften. Add the corn, salt and pepper and sauté briefly.

    3. Reduce the heat to simmer and add the cream and cheese pieces. Stir to melt the cheese and cook, uncovered for 5 minutes.

    4. Serve immediately. Serves 4 to 6.

Calabacitas con Queso y Chile Verde
(Zucchini with cheese and green chile)

    2 green onions or ½ small onion,
      chopped
    1 medium tomato, peeled and chopped
    1 tablespoon oil or shortening
    2 or more large, mild green chiles,
      roasted, peeled, cleaned and
      chopped (or 2 or more canned
      green chiles, coarsely chopped)
      Generous pinch of oregano
    ½ teaspoon salt
    2 to 3 tablespoons water
    1 pound zucchini, in bite-size pieces
    3 or 4 ounces Monterey jack
      cheese, grated

    1. Sauté slightly all the ingredients except the cheese and zucchini.

    2. Add 2 to 3 tablespoons water to the cooked mixture, and then the zucchini. Simmer until the squash is tender.

    3. Add cheese without mashing the zucchini. (This recipe is equally good with summer squash, chayote squash, or green beans.) Serve hot. Serves 4 to 6.

Coliflor con Salsa de Jalapeños Rojos
(Cauliflower with red jalapeño sauce)

    1 large head cauliflower
    1 recipe Salsa de Jalapeños Rojos,
      page 27 or Salsa Frita, page 26
    2 ounces queso fresco or feta cheese,
      crumbled

    1. Break the cauliflower into flowerets and steam; do not overcook.

    2. Top with warmed salsa and sprinkle with the crumbled cheese. (For variety, zucchini may be substituted for the cauliflower.) Serves 6.

Ejotes y Papas
(Green beans and potatoes)

    1 pound green beans
    6 small red potatoes
    ½ cup vinegar and oil dressing,
      page 77 or vinaigrette, page 60

    1. Snip the ends from the green beans, and leave them whole. Cut the potatoes in half (quarter if they are large).

    2. Place the potatoes on the bottom of a large pot or steam basket. Lay the green beans on top. Steam until barely tender, approximately 15 minutes. The vegetables must remain slightly firm.

    3. Place the vegetables into a bowl and pour the dressing over all. Refrigerate 3 hours. Serve chilled. Serves 6.

Habas
(Fava beans)

This recipe uses the fresh fava bean which resembles a large overgrown green bean. Snap the bean pod and remove the beans from inside. They will be the approximate size of a large lima bean.

    4 to 5 pounds fava beans in the pod;
      or 1½ pounds, shelled.
    2 tomatoes, broiled and peeled
    1 clove garlic, minced
    1 teaspoon salt
    ⅛ teaspoon oregano
    2 tablespoons lard
    ½ onion, chopped

    1. Remove the fava beans from their pods, cover with boiling water and allow to stand for an hour.

    2. Remove the skin from each bean. Barely cover the beans with water, bring to a boil, cover and simmer until fork tender, about 15 minutes.

    3. Broil the tomatoes until fork tender, about 15 minutes. Cool and peel.

    4. Place the tomatoes, garlic, salt and oregano in the blender. Blend briefly on low speed to an even consistency.

    5. Melt the lard in a skillet, sauté the onion until soft. Add the tomato purée and cook over high heat for 2 minutes. Slowly add the cooking liquid from the beans (there should be about 1½ cups). Bring to a boil, reduce heat to simmer, add the beans and simmer 5 to 10 minutes. Serves 6.

Avocado

Back in the 1940s the buttery textured avocado was still a novelty to most of the U.S. except the southwest and west. The bland taste still leaves some people less than enthusiastic. But it is widely used in Mexican cookery and its versatility is verified by the fact that there are entire cookbooks devoted to the fruit, including everything from soup to avocado ice cream. It's best known and most popular use is in Mexican guacamole — mashed avocados with chiles, tomatoes, and onions. Guacamole itself is versatile, too. It is used as a salad, a filler for burritos, a sandwich spread or as a meat sauce.

Guacamole I
(Avocado salad)

    2 ripe avocados
    1 small tomato, chopped
    1 tablespoon onion, minced
      Dash or two of garlic powder
    2 or more canned green chiles, seeded
      and chopped
      Lemon juice to taste (optional)
      Salt and pepper to taste
      Paprika

    1. Halve the avocados. Remove the seed. Scoop out pulp and mash with a fork.

    2. Add the other ingredients. Season to taste.

    3. Put in small serving bowl. Sprinkle with paprika for color.

    4. Cover well and chill until needed. Makes about 2 cups.

Guacamole II
(Avocado with sour cream)

This guacamole is similar to the others, but is milder since it contains no chiles.

2 large avocados, peeled and
   coarsely mashed
2 teaspoons lemon juice
⅓ cup sour cream
1 small clove garlic, crushed
1 teaspoon salt
1 tomato, diced
½ onion, minced
   Few sprigs cilantro, slightly chopped

Combine ingredients in order given. Stir briefly after adding each ingredient. Makes about 2½ cups.

Guacamole is very versatile. It may be used with the addition of chile as a *salsa*; puréed thick as a dip; puréed thin as a sauce (by adding ¼ cup half-and-half to the above recipe), served as a salad, or used with a combination of other vegetables.

Guacamole con Tomatillos

(*Guacamole* with Mexican green tomatoes)
In this recipe, a very different taste is supplied by the *tomatillos* and *cilantro*.

4 or 5 fresh or canned *tomatillos*
2 or more canned green chiles, seeded
   (or 1 *serrano* or *jalapeño* chile, if
   hotter sauce is desired)
2 ripe avocados
1 tablespoon onion, minced
   Salt and pepper
   Fresh cilantro leaves, minced
   (for garnish)

1. If using fresh *tomatillos,* discard husks and wash *tomatillos.* Boil in a small amount of water until just tender, about 5 minutes. Drain. Combine *tomatillos* and chiles in a blender. (If using one of the hotter chiles, discard stem and seeds first.)

2. Halve the avocados, remove seed. Scoop out pulp and mash with a fork. Add other ingredients. Mix well and season with salt and pepper. Sprinkle cilantro over top. Cilantro is very strong in taste. Use with caution. Make about 2½ cups.

Ensalada de Pimientos

(Pimiento salad)
This dish is most often prepared with red pimientos (*pimientos morones*) but it's even more colorful to use red and green bell peppers.

1 pound red pimientos (or combination
   of red and green bell peppers)
1 small onion, sliced into thin rounds
1 tomato, in half slices
3 tablespoons olive oil
2 tablespoons vinegar
   Salt and pepper to taste

1. Scorch the pimientos or bell peppers thoroughly over an open flame or in a broiler. As they are done, put them in a paper bag to steam. After a few minutes they should peel easily.

2. Cut off the stems and remove the seeds. Cut into narrow strips and arrange on a serving platter. Top with onion rounds. Surround with the half slices of tomato.

Guacamole, *the all purpose unguent smooths the way for many things, as an appetizer, salad or sauce.*

3. Mix the oil, vinegar, salt and pepper, and pour over the peppers. Serves 4.

Oil and Vinegar Dressing

1 clove garlic, crushed
¼ cup white wine vinegar
1 teaspoon salt
¾ cup oil (half olive oil, half salad oil)
½ teaspoon pepper
½ teaspoon dry or Dijon mustard

1. Combine garlic, vinegar and salt in a jar. Shake until the salt dissolves.

2. Add remaining ingredients and shake until thoroughly blended. Yield, about 1 cup dressing.

Escabeche de Cebolla

(Pickled onion)
Pickled onions are one of the most important garnishes for Mexican food. Red onions are especially attractive prepared this way.

2 white or red onions, thinly sliced
¼ teaspoon peppercorns
2 tablespoons cilantro leaves
   or ¼ teaspoon oregano
3 cloves garlic, peeled and sliced
½ teaspoon salt
   Vinegar to cover (use either white
   wine vinegar diluted with equal parts
   water or full strength rice wine
   vinegar)

In a quart jar, mix all ingredients together and refrigerate. Make at least one day ahead. Improves as it seasons.

A different onion garnish that is ready sooner is prepared by Josefina Rhodes using white onions:

Cover thinly sliced white onions with boiling water. Let stand for 10 minutes. Drain and cool. Toss with a little oregano, lime juice and salt. Serve as a garnish.

Ensalada de Calabacitas
(Zucchini salad)

2 pounds small zucchini, peeled
½ white onion, thinly sliced
3 large, mild green chiles roasted,
 peeled, cleaned, cut into thin strips
1 can (2 oz.) sliced ripe olives
⅓ cup oil and vinegar dressing, page 77
1 avocado, peeled and cubed
3 ounces *queso fresco* or feta
 cheese, crumbled

1. Steam the zucchini whole, do not overcook. Cut the zucchini into ½-inch slices.

2. Combine with the onion, chiles, olives and pour dressing over all.

3. Refrigerate at least 2 hours to thoroughly chill.

4. Stir in avocado pieces and top with crumbled cheese. Serves 6.

Plátanos
(Plantains, cooking bananas)
Bananas are available in great variety in Mexico — long, short, fat, skinny, green, yellow, red and black. The cooking bananas usually are called *plátanos machos* (plantains). These are becoming increasingly available in our markets. Generally fatter than the common banana, they may be marketed from their green stage through yellow to black. The green ones ripen quickly in a warm room and are ready to cook when black and soft to the touch. Common bananas may be substituted in these recipes, but should be used before they are fully ripe.

Plátanos Fritos
(Fried bananas)
Slice the peeled bananas either into half-inch rings, or slice lengthwise and cut into sections. Fry in butter until tender and golden brown. Salt lightly and serve as you would French fried potatoes.

Plátanos Dulces
(Sweet bananas)

3 *plátanos* (plantains or cooking
 bananas)
2 tablespoons butter
2 tablespoons brown sugar
 Powdered cinnamon
2 ounces white wine

Slice each banana in half lengthwise. Sauté in the butter until golden brown and tender. Sprinkle the brown sugar over the bananas, along with some powdered cinnamon. Add the white wine and simmer gently until the wine is absorbed. The banana pieces should not be too dry. Serve as a substitute for sweet potatoes or yams. As a dessert, omit cinnamon. Top instead with whipped cream flavored with sugar and powdered ginger at time of serving. Serves 2 to 3.

Bananas and plantains come in many kinds and colors in markets of Mexico.

Frijoles
(Beans)
We had really never considered the idea of cooking *frijoles,* Mexican beans, in a pressure cooker until we tasted some that Noemi Quiroga cooked that way.

The very idea was a bit outrageous; even the most liberated cookbook writers still swear by the crockery bean pot and long, slow cooking. But careful, multiple, blindfold taste-tests with experienced bean lovers have convinced us that pressure-cooked beans are indistinguishable from slow-cooked beans in flavor. Differences in texture seem apparent to the eye and come from stirring and tasting the slow-cooked beans. If you know your beans, you can time them to a tee in your pressure cooker; if in doubt, undercook a bit and finish with the lid off.

The fact is, we enjoy the slow way in a handsome old *olla* and the habit is too ingrained to change now.

Frijoles de Olla
(Beans from the pot)

2 cups dry pinto beans
8 to 10 cups water
2 tablespoons lard or oil
1 tablespoon salt
 Garnishes: Chile *salsa* or minced onion
 or sour cream; grated *queso añjo* or
 Monterey jack cheese

1. Pick through and wash the beans. Do not soak.

2. Place beans, water and lard in a large pot. Bring to a boil, cover and simmer 2¼ hours.

3. Add the salt and continue to cook ½ hour longer.

4. Garnish and serve in small bowls with their own broth.

Makes approximately 6 cups beans.

Frijoles Negros
(Black beans)

1 pound black beans (2¼ cups)
8 cups water
2 tablespoons lard or oil
1 tablespoon salt
2 sprigs fresh *epazote* if available
 Garnishes: Small wedges of cream
 cheese or sour cream; finely minced
 onion, and optional chile *rajas* (strips)

1. Pick through and wash the beans. Do not soak.

2. Place the beans, water and lard in a large pot. Bring to a boil, cover and gently simmer for 2 hours.

3. Add the salt and *epazote* and continue to simmer, covered, for 1 hour.

4. Serve in a small bowl with some of the bean broth and above garnishes, or drain (reserving some broth) and use for *frijoles refritos.* Makes 6 cups beans.

Noemi's Pressure Cooked Beans

2 cups pinto beans
8 cups water
1 tablespoon salt
2 tablespoons lard or oil

1. Pick through and wash the beans.

2. Bring the 8 cups of water to a boil in the pressure cooker. Add the beans and bring to a boil. Boil for 5 minutes, remove from the heat, cover and let stand for at least 1 hour.

3. Add the salt and lard and cook at 15 pounds pressure for 10 minutes. Allow pressure to drop normally.

4. Serve with a sprinkle of crushed oregano, chopped green onions and shredded longhorn or Monterey jack cheese. Makes approximately 6 cups beans.

Frijoles Refritos
(Well-fried beans)

4 to 5 cups cooked beans (pinto, black,
 pink, or small red)
¼ cup lard or oil
1 clove garlic, crushed (optional)
 Queso fresco (cheese)
 Ground avocado leaf (optional)
8 to 10 tortillas

1. Reserve broth from cooked beans.

2. In a heavy skillet, heat the lard until it smokes; lower the heat. Add 1 cup beans and mash thoroughly.

3. Add the garlic and stir.

4. Add the additional beans, approximately 1 cup at a time, mashing thoroughly between each addition.

5. Reduce heat and allow the beans to cook into a thick paste. If too dry, stir in small amounts of the reserved bean broth.

6. Serve as a side dish or separate *frijoles* course, garnished with *queso fresco* or toasted, ground avocado leaf; or spread the bean paste onto prepared *tostadas*. Makes 8 to 10 *tostadas*. Serves 6 as a side dish.

To prepare avocado leaf: Lightly toast fresh or dried avocado leaves on a preheated *comal*. Grind into a fine powder.

Jícama

The *jícama* is a brown-skinned root vegetable common all over Mexico and Central America. It looks very much like a sugar beet, with an interior much like that of an apple in texture and color. It cooks well, and can be used in soups and stews, but it is more often used raw. It is also common in Chinese foods, as a substitute for water chestnut, which it resembles in taste.

Ensalada de Jícama
(*Jícama* salad)

1 small (½ lb.) *jícama*, peeled and diced
1 bell pepper, seeded and chopped, or thinly sliced
1 cup cucumber, sliced or chopped
1 small onion, thinly sliced
2 tablespoons wine vinegar
¼ cup olive oil
½ teaspoon crushed oregano
Salt and pepper

1. Combine the cut vegetables.

2. Mix the other ingredients and pour the dressing over the vegetables.

3. Serve on a lettuce leaf. Serves 4.

Ensalada de Jícama y Naranjas
(*Jícama* and orange salad)
This is our favorite *jícama* salad. Even made a day in advance the *jícama* stays crisp and crunchy.

1 small (½ lb.) *jícama*, peeled and diced
½ cucumber, thinly sliced
1 small onion, thinly sliced
2 or 3 oranges, peeled and thinly sliced
¼ cup olive or other salad oil
⅓ cup wine vinegar
½ teaspoon salt
Lettuce

1. Mix the sliced vegetables and oranges.

2. Top with a dressing made from the oil, vinegar, and salt.

Serves as a salad on iceberg or romaine lettuce. Serves 4 to 6.

Jícama con Chile y Limón
(*Jícama* with chile and lime)
This is the most common way to eat *jícama,* popular on the streets of Mexico where it is sold from little carts

The colorful Ensalada de Noche Buena *salad is traditionally served on Christmas eve.*

or stands. As *jícamas* come in sizes from less than ½ pound to several pounds, be sure to buy the amount to fit your needs.

1 tablespoon salt
½ to 1 teaspoon powdered chile, mild or not, according to taste
1 small *jícama*, peeled and cut into small wedges
2 limes or lemons, cut into wedges

1. Mix the salt and chile powder in a small bowl, or preferably, have salt and powdered chile available in separate shakers.

2. Arrange *jícama* on toothpicks and lime wedges on a platter.

3. To eat, rub or squeeze lime over the *jícama,* then dip the moistened *jícama* into the salt and chile mixture, or use the shakers. Serves 6.

Pico de Gallo
(Rooster's beak)
This combination is called rooster's beak, supposedly because it was commonly eaten with finger and thumb, suggesting the pecking of a rooster. It makes a good toothpick hors d'oeuvre.

1 *jícama,* peeled and cut into small wedges
3 oranges, peeled and cut into thin slices or bite-size pieces
Powdered chile, mild or hot, according to taste
Salt

The *jícama* and oranges can be arranged ahead of time on a tray with salt and chile shakers so the guests can flavor to their taste. Serves 6.

Ensalada de Noche Buena
(Christmas Eve salad)

8 ounces diced beets (optional)
2 oranges, peeled, sliced and quartered
1 large *jícama*, peeled and cubed
3 slices fresh pineapple, cubed
½ head iceberg lettuce, shredded
2 bananas, sliced
½ cup peanuts, unsalted
Seeds from 1 pomegranate

1. In a bowl, mix together, beets, oranges, *jícama,* and pineapple. Refrigerate to thoroughly chill.

2. Line a salad bowl or platter with the shredded lettuce.

3. Mix bananas into the fruit mixture.

4. Place on lettuce and garnish with peanuts and pomegranate seeds. Serves 6 to 8.

Chile con Queso
(Chiles with cheese)

This dish is popular throughout the southwest U. S., and is usually made with yellow cheese. You may substitute a mild cheddar to replace the cream cheese, if you wish.

---

3 tablespoons butter
1 onion, finely chopped
3 tomatoes, peeled and chopped
4 mild green chiles, roasted, peeled, cleaned and torn into thin strips
¼ teaspoon salt
¼ teaspoon pepper
½ cup half-and-half
½ pound cream cheese, cut into small pieces

---

1. In a skillet, melt the butter, add the onion and cook until soft. Add the tomatoes, chiles, salt, pepper and cook uncovered over medium heat for 10 minutes.

2. Reduce the heat and add the half-and-half; when the cream is heated through, add the cheese pieces. Continue to cook, stirring until the cheese is melted and the mixture is thick, approximately 10 minutes. Serve warm. Serves 4 to 6.

Serving Suggestions:

As an *antojito:* serve with small *sopaipillas* or *totopos.*

As a vegetable: to accompany plain meats (grilled, roasted or barbecued).

As a brunch: accompanied by *frijoles refritos* and hot, soft *tortillas.*

Chiles rellenos

Chiles rellenos are a simple touch-stone to define excellence in a Mexican kitchen. There are three distinct schools of thought on the egg batter that cloaks the chile, that in turn envelops the cheese or other goodies inside. This batter may be flat, fluffy or super fluffy. Our recipes are right in the middle. If you want flatter *chiles rellenos,* just beat the eggs without separating them. If you prefer them fluffier, follow the recipe, but fold in 1 tablespoon flour for *each* egg.

Chiles Rellenos
(Stuffed chiles)

---

6 large, mild green chiles, roasted and peeled
½ pound Monterey jack or longhorn cheese, grated or in strips
Flour
3 eggs, separated
Salt and pepper to taste
Oil for frying

---

1. Leave stems on chiles for easy handling. Slit each chile down one side carefully, remove seeds and veins.

2. Stuff with some of the cheese. Dust each chile with a little flour and lay aside until the egg is ready.

3. Beat the whites of the eggs until stiff, fold in the lightly beaten yolks, and season to taste.

4. Heat ¼ inch oil in a skillet. Drop a large spoonful of the egg mixture into the skillet; lay a stuffed chile in the middle of the egg mixture. Top and enclose with another spoonful of egg. Turn and cook until golden brown. Serve hot immediately, topped with heated *salsa.* Serves 4 to 6.

Salsa

---

1 small onion finely chopped
1 clove garlic, minced
2 tablespoons lard or oil
2 large tomatoes, peeled and chopped
2 green chiles, chopped (for mild sauce) or 1 or more *serrano* or *jalapeño* chiles, chopped (for a sauce with more bite)
1 teaspoon salt
Cilantro, chopped parsley or pinch of oregano (optional)

Sauté the onions and garlic in the oil until soft. Add the other ingredients and cook for another 5 minutes over a low heat. Serve hot. A sprig of chopped cilantro or parsley, or a generous pinch of crushed oregano may be added just before serving. Serves 4 to 6.

Variation: *Chiles rellenos* may be made ahead and reheated in the following broth.

---

1 tablespoon lard or oil
½ cup onion, chopped
2 cloves garlic, crushed
1 can (28 ozs.) solid pack tomatoes (3½ cups, puréed in the blender)
3½ cups chicken stock
1½ teaspoons salt
¼ to ½ cup cilantro leaves, slightly chopped

---

1. Heat the lard in a large pot. Add the onion and garlic and cook only until the onion is soft.

2. Add the puréed tomatoes, chicken stock and salt. Bring to a boil. Reduce heat and simmer 5 minutes.

3. Add cilantro and the stuffed chiles. Simmer only to heat thoroughly. Serves 4 to 6.

Chiles Rellenos de Elote
(Chiles stuffed with fresh corn)

Most Americans are never exposed to any *chiles rellenos* except those stuffed with cheese. If you are serving other Mexican food with cheese, substitute another filling for *chiles rellenos.* Try one of the following: fresh corn, tuna or canned sardines with minced onion, *picadillo,* either meat or chicken.

---

6 green chiles, seeded
4 ears corn, kernels cut from cob (or canned kernel corn, drained)
2 eggs
2 ounces grated Parmesan or Romano cheese
½ teaspoon salt
½ cup light cream

Select young, firm nopales *(cactus leaves).*

Prepare chiles as for *chiles rellenos.* Grind the corn in blender. Mix ground corn with the lightly beaten eggs, half of the grated cheese, and salt. Stuff the chiles with the egg and corn mixture and arrange in a baking dish. Top with the cream and the remaining cheese. Bake at 350 degrees for about 25 minutes. Serves 6.

Chiles en Nogada
(Chiles in creamed walnut sauce)

Nogada, a cream and walnut sauce, is one of the famous sauces of Mexico, generally served over chiles stuffed with a *picadillo* of chicken or pork. It is served on patriotic occasions such as the *Cinco de Mayo,* or on the Sixteenth of September, which commemorates the beginning of the Mexican fight for independence from Spain in 1810. The theme is carried out by serving the white *nogada* garnished with pomegranate seeds and sprigs of parsley or cilantro; the red, white and green represent the flag of Mexico.

Nogada

---

1 cup walnuts, pecans or almonds
1 tablespoon sugar
4 tablespoons warm water
½ cup dry bread crumbs
1 tablespoon vinegar
Light cream, about 1 cup
1 pomegranate, or canned spiced crab apples
Sprigs of parsley or cilantro

---

1. Purée the walnuts or other nuts in a blender or chop very fine.

2. Soak nuts in sugar and water. Add the bread crumbs and let stand for about 15 minutes before adding vinegar.

3. Add light cream to attain desired consistency, (thin enough to pour) just before pouring over the *chiles rellenos.*

Trim the spines from the nopales.

Dice the nopales *into ½ inch pieces.*

Cook in boiling, salted water until tender.

Picadillo fillings:

Fillings for *chiles rellenos* with *nogada* sauce can be sweet or not, according to personal preference. Any kind of a meat mixture that is not too strong in taste is satisfactory.

Picadillo de Puerco (Chopped pork hash)

1 pound lean pork, coarsely chopped
  Salt
1 small onion, chopped
1 clove garlic, minced
1 tomato, peeled and chopped
1 teaspoon sugar
¼ cup ripe olives, chopped
1 apple, peeled, cored and chopped
¼ cup almonds, chopped
¼ cup seedless raisins, plumped in hot
  water and drained
⅛ teaspoon cinnamon
⅛ teaspoon ground cloves

1. In a skillet add enough boiling water to barely cover the pork. Season with salt. Cover and cook until meat is tender. Remove cover and simmer until liquid has evaporated.

2. Add onion, garlic and tomato and cook for another 5 or 6 minutes.

3. Add the rest of the ingredients, season to taste, and cook for 2 minutes more. Mixture should be fairly dry.

4. Use hot as a filling for *chiles rellenos.* This is enough filling for 6 to 8 chiles.

Picadillo de Pollo (Chicken hash)

2 cups cooked chicken, shredded
1 tablespoon oil
1 small onion finely chopped
1 clove garlic, minced
2 carrots, diced
1 cup peas
1 potato, diced
1 teaspoon sugar (optional)
¼ cup seedless raisins
  Small sprigs parsley, or cilantro
⅛ teaspoon cinnamon
⅛ teaspoon ground cloves
1 cup chicken stock or broth
  Salt and pepper to taste

1. Sauté the shredded chicken in the oil with the onions and garlic until the vegetables are soft but not brown.

2. Add the rest of the ingredients and simmer in chicken stock for about 15 minutes or until the liquid is almost absorbed.

3. Use hot as a filling for *chiles rellenos.* Makes enough filling for 6 to 8 chiles.

To Serve *Chiles En Nogada*

1. Stuff the chiles with the hot .*picadillo* of your choice and arrange on a serving dish.

2. Spoon the cold *nogada* sauce over each chile.

3. Garnish with sprigs of parsley or fresh cilantro. Though the authentic way to provide the red for the color scheme is with pomegranate seeds, we prefer to use drained slices of spiced crab apple. Sometimes the stuffed chiles are covered with batter and fried, but we prefer them uncooked.

Nopalitos
(Cactus leaves)

The leaves or pads of the prickly pear cactus are widely used in Mexico in stews, soups, with eggs, or cold in salads. In this country, they are sold in their raw state in groceries in the southwest and sometimes in the vegetable sections of supermarkets. They may also be purchased in jars as *nopalitos* (from the Spanish *nopal,* or cactus.)

The pads of prickly pear plants vary considerably in the number and sharpness of their spines. Those with very sharp spines must be handled with tongs and with great care. The *Opuntia basilaris* is a nearly thornless variety that is easiest to handle. (See photos above.)

To prepare raw cactus pads, cut away stickers, dice and simmer in salted water until tender. Drain in a colander with a damp towel over the top to prevent excess solidification of the juices, which are slippery like okra. The canned *nopalitos* should be rinsed in cold water before using to eliminate the slippery juice. The taste and texture is somewhat like green beans, with a tartness that is quite special. (See also, page 17.)

Ensalada de Nopalitos
(Cactus salad)

1 jar (16 to 20 oz.) *nopalitos*
3 tablespoons white onion, finely
  chopped
3 medium tomatoes, blanched, peeled,
  seeded and chopped
½ teaspoon salt, or to taste
  Oil and vinegar dressing
1 tablespoon (or more) cilantro,
  chopped

1. Rinse the cactus pieces in cold water and drain.

2. Mix with the other ingredients, and add the dressing to taste. Garnish with chopped cilantro. Serves 6.

Ensalada de Chayote
(*Chayote* salad)

3 *chayotes*
1 small white onion, thinly sliced
2 tomatoes, halved and cut into wedges
1 can (2 oz.) sliced olives
⅓ cup oil and vinegar dressing, page 77
⅓ cup cilantro leaves
  Iceberg lettuce, shredded

1. Cut *chayotes* in half, peel and steam approximately 15 minutes. Be careful not to overcook.

2. Chop the *chayote* into chunky bite-size pieces.

3. In a bowl, combine all ingredients, except lettuce. Toss and refrigerate to marinate at least 1 hour.

4. Serve on a bed of shredded lettuce. Serves 6.

Fruits and sweets

The pre-Hispanic Mexicans had very few cakes, candies and desserts — the natural bounty of fruits was apparently sufficient. But never underestimate the ability of a culture to embrace and elaborate upon whatever new sweets are offered.

Some of the favorite fruits of Mexico are grown in or imported by the U.S — the papaya, mango, orange and coconut. All these, along with the gorgeous slices of melons and pineapples, are sold as snacks by street vendors all over Mexico, as are the less familiar *guavas, sapotes, guanabanas, tunas, cherimoyas,* tamarinds and *mameys.*

Desserts, as such, were not a part of the native culture of Mexico. Most Mexicans are still not great dessert eaters, but many sweets are consumed between meals. The cakes, custards, and pastries that now compete with the luscious fruits of the Mexican table were introduced by the Spanish nuns. These were usually served as special treats created for religious holidays or other important occasions. Most Mexican desserts and sweets are modifications of Spanish and French desserts. Many of them even preserve their Spanish names, although many, due to the inclusion of native fruits, must be considered truly Mexican. Luckily for visitors, after a full Mexican dinner, the dessert is often a small portion or just a piece of fruit.

The Mexican taste for sweets is strong, or at least it likes to concentrate its sweets and observes no strict line between candies and desserts. Visitors often find commercial soft drinks and candies too sweet.

Sugar cane was brought into Mexico soon after the conquest by Hernando Cortés in 1521. By 1524, a sugar refinery was operating in the south of Mexico. The native sweets

◁

Fresh fruits and melons are the favored desserts and snacks, in the market, and at home.

that are least expensive and most popular are often "chews" of green sugar cane, baked hearts of *maguey,* tamarind pulp, and the pods from the *huamuchil* tree.

Flan
(Caramel-coated custard)

Caramel:
½ cup sugar
2 tablespoons water
Custard:
2 cups milk
½ cup sugar
4 eggs
1 teaspoon vanilla
Pinch of salt

1. Choose a one-quart mold with a smooth inside surface, or use 6 individual molds.

2. To caramelize mold: In a small saucepan, over high heat, boil ½ cup sugar with 2 tablespoons water. When golden, pour into mold, turning quickly in all directions to coat bottom and sides.

3. Custard: In a blender put milk, sugar, eggs, vanilla, and salt. Blend 3 minutes on medium speed.

4. Pour into mold. Place the mold in a larger pan. Pour warm water into the larger pan halfway up the sides of the mold. (In Spanish this is *Baño de Maria,* Mary's Bath).

5. Bake at 325 degrees in a preheated oven for about 1 hour. Check occasionally during the baking to be sure the *Baño de Maria* does not boil. If it should, reduce oven heat slightly; however, do not reduce below 300 degrees.

6. Test for doneness by inserting a kitchen knife only halfway into the custard. (Do not pierce bottom.) If the knife comes out clean, it's done. Cool 1 hour and refrigerate at least 3 hours.

7. Unmold by running a kitchen knife around the edge. Place a serving dish over the mold and flip. Serves 6.

Helado de Mango
(Mango ice)

2 cans (15 oz. each) sliced,
sweetened mangos
Juice of 1 lime
Pinch salt
Water
½ cup sugar, more or less to taste
Coarse crushed ice (7 pounds)
Rock salt
Ice cream maker

1. Drain and reserve the liquid from the mangos. Place the mango pieces, juice of 1 lime, and pinch of salt in the blender. Blend until smooth.

2. Measure the mango pulp. Add water to the reserved mango liquid to equal the mango pulp. Combine pulp, liquid and sugar; mix well.

3. Freeze in an ice cream maker, following manufacturer's directions. Ices require approximately one quarter more rock salt for the brine than does ice cream (1¼ part rock salt to 4 parts ice). Serves 4 to 6.

Both the Mexican "sweet tooth" and flair for color are displayed in this candy shop in Mercado Libertad.

Waitresses in Puerto Vallarta seem to enjoy sampling their own merchandise.

Capirotada
(Mexican bread pudding)

Although the name is Spanish in origin, the meat-based dish of Spain has little in common with the Mexican *capirotada*. It is one of Mexico's most popular Lenten dishes and one of the most exciting and tempting desserts of the world.

This recipe uses walnuts, but in Mexico, peanuts, pine nuts, or almonds are often used instead. Apple slices may also be included. Prunes or other dried fruit can be used instead of, or with, the raisins.

The most important ingredient is the bread, which must be absolutely dry. It should be sliced, cubed, and dried in a shallow baking pan in a slow oven, but not toasted. Sweet French bread, not sourdough, is best.

- 4 cups *piloncillo* or brown sugar
- 2 whole cloves
- 2 pieces stick cinnamon, each about two inches in length
- ¼ pound butter
- 2 quarts boiling water
- 2 loaves sweet French bread, oven dried, and cubed
- 2 cups walnuts, peanuts or almonds, chopped
- 2 cups seedless raisins, rinsed in hot water, and drained
- ½ pound *each* Monterey jack cheese and longhorn cheese, grated

1. Add the *piloncillo*, cloves, cinnamon, and butter to the boiling water and allow to simmer until a light syrup forms. Remove the cloves and cinnamon.

2. In a large, buttered, baking dish, layer the dry bread cubes, nuts, raisins, and mixed grated cheeses until all the ingredients are used. Now spoon the hot syrup evenly over the bread mixture.

3. Bake in a preheated oven at 350 degrees for 30 minutes. Serve either hot or cold. Serves 12.

Plátanos Borrachos de Yucatán
(Drunken bananas from the Yucatán)

- 3 *plátanos* (plantain or cooking bananas)
- 2 tablespoons butter, melted
- ¼ cup flour
- ¼ cup powdered sugar
- 1 orange, peeled and sliced
- 4 ounces rum
- Juice of 1 lemon
- 1 tablespoon sugar
- 4 tablespoons water

1. Peel the bananas. With a pastry brush, coat them with butter. Roll in a mixture of the flour and powdered sugar.

2. Put the bananas in a low, buttered baking dish. Arrange the orange slices over the bananas. Combine rum, lemon juice, sugar and water and pour over fruit.

3. Bake in a 350 degree oven for 25 minutes. Serves 6.

Churros
(Spanish doughnuts)

Churros are a traditional Spanish food which also has become Mexican. In Spanish cities there are *churrerías* or *churro* stands, and at all festivals a common sight is the *churro* maker with his great cauldron of boiling oil, selling his wares in long ropes of tasty brown dough.

The *churros* sold on the street are simple blends of flour, water and salt, seldom including the eggs that are usually added in home kitchens. They are especially good served with the wonderful Mexican hot chocolate.

Churros are made of heavy, semi-cooked dough forced through the ornamental slots of a *churrera* (a special utensil like a heavy cake decorator). A wooden plunger is used to push the dough in long strips into the boiling oil. If you don't have a *churrera*, use your cake decorator, using the largest hole or a pastry bag with a #6 star tip.

- Oil to cover for deep frying
- 1 cup water
- 1 tablespoon oil
- 1 tablespoon sugar
- ¼ teaspoon cinnamon
- ½ teaspoon salt
- 1 cup sifted flour
- 1 egg
- Powdered sugar, or sugar and cinnamon

1. Heat oil in deep fryer or pan before beginning to mix the *churros*. The oil should be starting to smoke (370 degrees).

2. Boil water. Add oil, sugar, cinnamon, and salt. Then add flour all at once, stirring with a wooden spoon until dough is smooth and thick. Remove pan from the heat. Beat egg quickly into flour mixture and stir until smooth.

3. Force the heavy mixture through the hole in the *churrera* (or decorator or pastry bag) in long strips into the hot oil. Cook until well browned. Remove and drain. Serve hot, sprinkled with powdered sugar, or rolled in a sugar-and-cinnamon mixture, or even plain. Recipe makes enough for 4 persons, but be prepared to make more.

This neighborhood doughnut maker lifts a spiral of hot churros from boiling oil. He'll take it to the table, and cut it into short lengths for his customers.

Buñuelos *are fried in oil, and usually served with syrup or honey.*

Buñuelos
(Fritters)

4 cups flour
1 teaspoon salt
1 teaspoon baking powder
2 tablespoons sugar
⅓ cup margarine
2 eggs
1 cup milk
　Oil for frying, at least 1 inch deep
　Sugar mixture: ½ cup sugar,
　2 teaspoons cinnamon or pinch of
　powdered cloves

1. Stir dry ingredients together, set aside.

2. Melt margarine.

3. In a large bowl beat eggs, then mix in milk. Gradually stir in dry ingredients. When thoroughly mixed, add melted margarine and, with hands, work margarine into the dough.

4. Turn onto a lightly floured board and knead gently until smooth and elastic. Divide dough and roll into 30 to 50 balls. With a rolling pin, roll each ball into a thin circle.

5. Fry in hot oil (400 degrees to 425 degrees). Turn to brown on both sides. Drain on paper towels.

6. Sprinkle with sugar mixture. Best served while still warm. They may also be served with a syrup made of *piloncillo* or brown sugar, flavored with cinnamon or with cinnamon and cloves.

Dough may be refrigerated up to 2 days, tightly covered, and then rolled as needed. This recipe also may be cut in half. Makes 30 to 50 *buñuelos.*

Buñuelos de Molde
(Molded fritters)

Like regular *buñuelos,* these flaky goodies are most common during the Christmas season, but would be attractive and delicious for any party occasion. To make them, you need the long-handled molds which can be bought at Mexican stores. As an alternative, you can use the fancy molds used for Italian or Scandinavian pastries. The designs are different, but the results are the same.

　Oil for deep frying
2 cups milk
2 cups sifted flour
4 eggs
¼ cup sugar
½ teaspoon salt
　Cinnamon and sugar mixture, or
　brown sugar syrup flavored with
　cinnamon or anise

1. Heat oil in a pan to 375 degrees.

2. In a bowl combine milk and flour, and beat well. Add eggs, sugar, and salt, and mix again.

3. Heat the mold in the hot oil. Then dip the mold in the batter, gently shaking off excess. Put the mold back in the hot oil until the fritter is golden brown. Remove. Drain on a paper towel. Dust with mixture of sugar and cinnamon, or serve with a syrup of brown sugar or Mexican *piloncillo,* flavored with cinnamon or anise. Makes about 30 fritters.

Sopaipillas
(Fritters)

Sopaipillas are browned puffs of dough, like *buñuelos* without eggs. They are commonly served with anise or cinnamon-flavored syrups as dessert items. In New Mexico where they are popular, *sopaipillas* are usually eaten with honey. Large ones are even stuffed with *frijoles.* They can be used instead of corn chips with *guacamole* and other dips. They refrigerate well, so can be made in advance, and reheated when needed.

---

2 cups sifted flour
2 teaspoons baking powder
1 teaspoon salt
2 tablespoons lard or shortening
½ cup water
Oil for deep frying

1. Sift together flour, baking powder, and salt. Work in shortening and water. Knead well, then allow to stand in a covered bowl for about an hour.

2. Roll out small balls of the dough on a lightly floured board until they are about ⅛ to ¼ inch thick. Cut the dough into small triangles, diamonds, or squares. Make them larger if they're to be stuffed.

3. Deep fry at 400 to 425 degrees. Push the fritters down in the oil several times to assure even puffing. Turn once to brown on both sides. Drain on absorbent paper. Makes about 20 small puffs.

Rosquillas
(Doughnut-shaped cookies)

Anise-flavored *rosquillas* are popular cookies in Mexico at Christmas. Like most Mexican baked goods, these have their origins in Europe. This recipe is from Mrs. Roman Colbert, formerly of Cadiz, who prepares them for Christmas parties.

¼ cup light rum
¼ cup anise seeds
¼ cup olive oil
2 eggs
2 cups flour
½ cup sugar
2 teaspoons baking powder
Extra flour for fixing the dough
Olive oil or other salad oil for deep frying

1. Add rum to the anise seeds and let set for two hours or more.

2. Add the olive oil and eggs. Mix well. Mix flour, sugar and baking powder in a bowl. Add the liquid mixture. Form a dough and knead well. Gradually add extra flour until the dough no longer sticks to the hands. It is now ready for use, or can be stored in the refrigerator for later use, but must be at room temperature when ready to use.

3. Form small balls, about the size of a large olive. Roll between the hands to form a strip about the thickness of a pencil. Join the ends to form a circle about 2 inches in diameter. Drop in hot oil (about 375 degrees) in deep fryer. When brown on one side, turn over and brown other side. Drain on paper toweling. When cool, dip into confectioners sugar. Will make about 20 *rosquillas.*

Tamales

Here are three of the many possible variations of sweet *tamales.*

Tamales de Dulce
(Sweet *tamales*)

---

2 cups *masa harina*
½ cup sugar
¼ teaspoon salt
1½ teaspoons cinnamon
1½ teaspoons baking powder
¼ cup margarine
¼ cup lard
1½ cups chicken stock
1 cup almonds, sliced or slivered
1 cup raisins (or blackberries, fresh or frozen, sweetened with sugar)
1 package dried corn husks, soaked in hot water to soften

1. Stir together dry ingredients (*masa harina,* sugar, salt, cinnamon and baking powder).

2. Cream margarine and lard until fluffy. Gradually beat *masa harina* mixture and broth into the lard. Beat well for about 5 minutes. (A small test ball of the dough should rise in cold water.) Stir almonds into dough. If using raisins, mix into the dough. If using blackberries, reserve and use as a center filling.

3. Place 6 to 8 cups of water and a coin into the bottom of the steamer. Shake excess water from the softened corn husks. Line steamer with corn husks. Spread dough (approximately 2 tablespoons) evenly on the center of remaining husks. If using blackberries, place a spoonful of berries in center of dough. Roll and turn up. If necessary, roll in an additional husk, or tie with a piece of string to secure. Pack *tamales* into steamer as they are made. Surround with corn husks.

4. Top with terry toweling and secure lid. Bring to a boil over high heat. Reduce to medium and steam for 1½ to 2 hours. Remember to listen for the coin; it will let you "hear" the

water level. When the coin becomes silent the water level is too low and you must add more.

5. To reheat, place in greased frying pan over medium-low and heat through, turning occasionally. If preferred the *tamales* may be wrapped in foil and reheated in a 350 degree oven 20 to 30 minutes. Use foil method and add an additional 15 minutes to reheat. *Tamales* freeze well. Makes about 1 dozen small *tamales.*

Tamales de Nueces y Coco
(Walnut and coconut *tamales*)

½ pound lard or shortening
¼ cup cold water
2 pounds *masa*
1 cup beef or pork broth
½ cup sugar
½ teaspoon ground cinnamon or ground anise seed
½ cup shredded coconut
1 cup raisins
½ cup chopped walnuts
Salt to taste
1 pound corn husks

1. Beat shortening and cold water until the mixture is fluffy. Add the *masa* to the shortening and mix well, adding, little by little, either the broth (for the Walnut and Coconut *Tamales),* or the juice from the fruit (for the Fruit *Tamales*) until the mixture is the consistency of drop biscuit batter, spreadable, but not as liquid as pancake batter. The dough should float in water when tested.

2. Now add other ingredients and mix well.

3. Clean the corn husks in warm water and stand on end to drain. This can be done in advance but husks should still be soft and pliable.

4. Take about a heaping tablespoon of the prepared *masa* and place it just above the middle of the wide part of a corn husk.

5. Fold in the sides and then across the middle. Tie the open end with a strip of corn husk.

6. Steam the *tamales* for one hour over (but not in) boiling water. A colander in a large kettle of boiling water can be used to hold the *tamales.* Makes 2 dozen small *tamales.*

Tamales de Fruta
(Fruit *tamales*)

½ pound lard or shortening
¼ cup cold water
2 pounds *masa*
1 can (29 oz.) crushed pineapple or equivalent in fresh or frozen strawberries
½ cup sugar
Salt to taste
1 pound corn husks

Follow above directions for preparing *Tamales de Nueces y Coco.*

Even very small towns have a bakery. Here, the town baker of San Sebastian puts Pan Dulce *into her oven.*

Bakery goods

Even the smallest towns in Mexico seem to have a bakery, or at least a baker. You may have to inquire where to find it, since villages don't often put up signs, even for a restaurant or hotel.

Very little baking is done in the Mexican home, each neighborhood in the city having its own bakery. A great variety of sizes and shapes of *pan dulce* (sweet breads) are offered even by the smaller bakeries. The baker is a respected professional, addressed as *El Maestro,* and has an appreciative but critical clientele. There are usually several bakes each day, and you must time your purchases to coincide with the emergence of your favorite items from the oven.

The *pan dulce* has a light, bread-like texture; it comes in many sizes and shapes with different dry toppings. The bakery also makes cream-filled puff pastries; pumpkin and pineapple filled *empanadas;* large cookies; cheese and fruit filled tarts; and the *bolillo,* a dinner roll that is somewhat like a hardcrusted sweet French dinner roll.

Pies, as we know them, are not a part of Mexican cooking. Cakes are not made by the local bakery, but by special bakeries or the convent nearby. These cakes are usually very rich and moist; finely ground nuts are used as a major part of the flour. The single layer, glazed cake, such as the *Pastel de Pecana* (page 88), is very French.

In addition to the recipe for pecan cake, we have included a recipe for the popular *pan dulce,* since most of us are not fortunate enough to have a Mexican baker close by. Thanks to Lee Lampo, a bread specialist and close friend of Vicki Barrios, the *pan dulce* recipe has been adapted to home use and converted to a cold rise technique to make it convenient for the home baker with a busy schedule.

The *pan dulce* is prepared and then refrigerated for up to 24 hours before baking, so that you can do them in advance and still have fresh-from-the-oven sweet rolls. Vicki says, "I prepare a full course Mexican brunch on Christmas morning each year, and it's wonderful to have oven-ready *pan dulce* all set to go."

Pan Dulce
(Sweet bread)

Rolls:
3½ cups flour
  2 pkgs. active dry yeast
  1 teaspoon salt
  ½ cup sugar
  ½ cup powdered milk
  2 tablespoons shortening
  1 egg
1¼ cups hot tap water

1. Stir together 1 cup flour, yeast, salt, sugar and powdered milk. Add shortening, egg and hot water. Beat at medium speed for 2 minutes. Add another cup of flour and beat at high speed for 2 minutes. Stir in remaining flour (1½ cups), mixing well.

2. Turn onto lightly floured board. Dough will be soft and sticky. Do not knead; but slightly turn dough several times with a spatula to lightly coat with flour. Cover loosely with plastic wrap and allow to rest 20 minutes only. Meanwhile, grease baking sheets and make topping.

Topping:
½ cup margarine
½ cup sugar
¼ teaspoon salt
  Yolk of one egg
  1 teaspoon cinnamon or vanilla
⅔ cup flour

Cream margarine, sugar and salt. Add egg yolk and cinnamon or vanilla and blend. Add flour and mix well. Mixture will be crumbly.

To assemble:

1. Keeping hands floured, divide dough into 12 pieces and shape into round, flat buns. Place on greased baking sheets.

2. Divide topping evenly. Sprinkle the top of each bun and lightly press down topping.

3. Refrigerate 4 to 24 hours loosely covered with plastic. Uncover and set out while oven preheats.

4. Bake at 400 degrees, 15 minutes. Makes 12 rolls.

Empanadas
(Turnovers)

For the pastry dough see page 60. Fill with pumpkin or pineapple fillings.

Calabaza (Pumpkin)

**2 cups canned pumpkin (or yams or sweet potato cooked, mashed)
2 large or 4 small cones *piloncillo*, crushed (or ½ cup brown sugar)
½ teaspoon anise seed, or coarse ground nutmeg**

1. Cook all ingredients together over medium heat for 20 minutes.

2. Cool to handle easily and fill prepared pastry. Brush tops with egg white.

3. Bake in 400 degree oven for 15 minutes. Makes 16 four-inch *empanadas*.

Piña (Pineapple)

**1 can (20 oz.) unsweetened pineapple chunks, drained (reserve liquid)
2 tablespoons cornstarch
3 tablespoons sugar (or to taste)
½ cup sliced almonds
1 cup coconut, unsweetened and coarsely shredded**

1. Cut pineapple chunks in half.

2. Add water to reserved liquid from pineapple to make ¾ cup. Blend with cornstarch in a pan. Add sugar, pineapple chunks and bring to a boil over medium-high heat, stirring constantly. Reduce to simmer and allow to thicken.

3. Stir in almonds and coconut. Cool and fill prepared pastry.

4. Bake at 400 degrees for 15 minutes. Roll in sugar while still warm. Makes 16 four-inch *empanadas*.

Colorful beehives are at home under a Tabachin tree in bloom.

Chayotes Rellenos
(Filled *chayotes*)

**3 small *chayotes*
3 eggs
¾ cup sugar
1 teaspoon nutmeg
6 ounces (6 slices) pound or sponge cake
½ cup dry sherry
¾ cup raisins
½ cup almonds, finely ground
½ cup sliced almonds**

1. Scrub the *chayotes* and cut in half. Steam them until fork tender (about 15 minutes), be sure not to overcook. Allow to cool.

2. Carefully remove the *chayote* pulp from the peel, leaving an even, thin layer of pulp, to form a shell that will maintain its shape.

3. Place the eggs, sugar, nutmeg and the *chayote* pulp in the blender. Blend briefly.

4. Crumble the cake into a bowl. Add the *chayote* purée and mix well. Stir in the sherry and raisins. Mix in ½ cup ground almonds or enough to make a spoonable, loose mixture.

5. Place the *chayote* shells in a greased, shallow baking pan. Spoon the mixture into the *chayote* shells, top with sliced almonds and bake in 350 degree oven for 30 minutes. Serve warm or cold. May be made a day in advance. Serves 6.

Note: Place any leftover cake mixture into a greased baking dish and bake in 350 degree oven for 30 to 45 minutes (depends on depth of cake mixture). Spoon into dessert bowls and top with softly whipped, unsweetened cream.

Dulces de Jícama y Coco
(*Jícama* and coconut candies)

**1 small *jícama,* peeled and coarsely grated
2 ounces unsweetened coconut shredded
½ cup orange juice
8 ounces sugar**

1. Mix all the ingredients and cook over a low flame, stirring constantly. When the sugar and orange juice have been absorbed and the mixture is sticky, remove from the heat.

2. Form little mounds on a piece of foil. Allow to cool. Makes about 25 to 30 candies.

Miel
(Honey)

Bee keeping has been practiced in Mexico since long before the conquest. Beehives are still made in some Indian areas by hollowing out a section of log. The modern beehives you see along the road are usually painted in different colors so that the stacked units are like rainbow bands.

The Huichol Indians believe that bees were created by the gods of the sea to give men wax for candles that could be used when the wood torches were damp and would not light.

Honey is used to make glazes and toppings, and is a favorite with *buñuelos* and *sopaipillas*.

Pastel de Pecana
(Pecan cake with honey glaze)

**4 eggs, separated
½ cup unsalted butter, melted and cooled
½ teaspoon vanilla
⅔ cup sugar
Pinch of salt
⅔ cup pecans, finely ground
⅓ cup flour**

1. Lightly butter and flour one 8 or 9-inch round or square pan.

2. In a small bowl, beat the egg yolks, butter and vanilla. Add ⅓ cup sugar and beat until thick and creamy.

3. In a larger bowl, beat the egg whites with a pinch of salt until frothy. Continue to beat, adding the remaining sugar 2 tablespoons at a time until stiff peaks form.

4. Fold ⅓ of the stiff whites into the yolk mixture to lighten it. Fold the yolk mixture into the remaining whites, folding to fully incorporate the whites.

5. Combine the nuts and flour and sift ⅓ at a time gently over the egg mixture, folding after each addition. Any nut piece too large to sift may be folded in at the last or reground in the blender. Pour into buttered pan.

6. Bake in 350 degree oven 30 minutes for 8-inch pan, 25 minutes for 9-inch pan, 325 degrees for glass or dark pans. Let stand for 10 minutes, then turn out of pan onto a wire rack (top up). Cool 1 hour and glaze. Serves 6 to 8.

Honey Glaze:

**2 tablespoons butter
½ cup honey**

1. Melt butter in a saucepan, add the honey and bring to a frothy boil. Reduce heat to medium and allow to boil for 3 to 4 minutes.

2. Allow to cool slightly and pour over the cake while the glaze is still slightly warm, allowing it to drip down the sides. (If the glaze should cool too long and harden, just reheat, stirring constantly until able to pour.)

Note: As the glaze tends to be sticky, for easier and neater cutting, use a very sharp knife, warmed in hot water and dried before cutting.

Pastel de Pecana is made with finely ground nutmeats. It is very rich and very French in character.

Beverages

There are a bewildering variety of liquid refreshments served in Mexico. The country seems to have retained all the drinks of both Indian and Spanish tradition, as well as embracing foreign imports and inventing many new ones of their own.

Many of the traditional drinks of pre-Hispanic Mexico are still alive (and in some cases still kicking). Most of these are simple fruit juices, or infusions of various seeds and plants; but quite a few are mildly alcoholic. Some, like our apple cider, come in both a soft and hard version.

There is *pulque* from the maguey plant, *colonche* from cactus fruit, *tuba* from the coconut palm, *tepache* from pineapple, *coatepec* from orange juice, and a corn beer called *tesquino* made by the Huichol Indians.

Mexican beer, (the European, not the Huichol type) is our favorite beverage with most Mexican food.

Batidos

Batido means beaten or trodden, and is the name used for those beverages that are now usually made in the blender using fruits and melons. In Mexico, tropical fruits such as *mamey* or *guanabana* are used in addition to fruits and berries common to American fruitstands The fruit, minus skins and seeds is liquified in a blender and mixed with with water or milk, sugared to taste, chilled, and served. Use milk with bananas, either water or milk with ripe strawberries and cantaloupe, only water with pineapple and guavas. Watermelon will probably need no other liquid. Add a little lemon juice

◁

The fruits of tropical Mexico are converted into a great variety of drinks, and the blender has made it a lot easier to do. Photo above: These "piñas" are not pineapples, but the heart of the maguey plant, from which tequila is made.

to guava *licuada* or to cantaloupe *licuado* with water. Add sugar to taste, chill and serve.

Licuado de Papaya y Naranja
(Papaya and orange drink)

1 ripe papaya
1 cup orange juice
1 teaspoon lemon juice

Peel and seed the papaya and cut into chunks. Liquify with the orange and lemon juice in a blender. Chill and serve. No sugar should be necessary unless the orange lacks usual sweetness. Make about 2 cups.

Refresco de Piña
(Pineapple cooler)

1 ripe pineapple, peeled
1 quart water
Sugar, ½ cup or more

Chop pineapple into small bits or cut into chunks and blend for a moment in a blender. In a glass container, add the pineapple to one quart of water in which half of the sugar has been dissolved. Allow to steep for 2 to 3 hours. Then strain, add additional sugar to personal taste, chill, and serve. Makes 4 to 5 cups.

Licuados *come in exotic pastel shades.*

Coffee grows in the kitchen gardens of much of tropical Mexico.

Señorita Casimira Orozco Carillo roasts coffee picked from the family garden in Cuale, Jalisco.

Horchatas

Horchatas, drinks made from steeped nuts, grains, or a tuber called *chufa,* are common summer coolers in the south of Spain. They have become popular in Mexico as non-alcoholic beverages.

Horchata de Almendras
(Almond *horchata*)

1 cup blanched almonds
Large piece fresh lemon peel
2 quarts water
2 tablespoons lemon, orange, or other
fruit flavored liqueur (optional)

Grind the almonds. Soak ground almonds and lemon peel in water for 3 or 4 hours. Discard lemon peel. Strain liquid through a cloth napkin, squeezing the remaining pulp in the napkin to extract all the milky liquid. Add sugar and liqueur (if desired) to taste. Chill and serve over ice cubes. Makes 8 cups.

Horchata de Arroz
(Rice *horchata*)

1 cup rice, washed
2 quarts water
1 piece stick cinnamon
Sugar to taste

Soak rice in water for 3 hours so that rice will swell. Then add the cinnamon stick and simmer for ½ hour. Remove cinnamon. Cool; strain the rice mixture through a cloth napkin, squeezing to extract all the milky liquid. Add sugar to taste. Chill and serve over ice cubes.
Makes about 8 cups.

Variation:
Instead of, or in addition to, the cinnamon, *horchata* may be flavored with other extracts or spices, or blended in a blender with fresh or frozen strawberries or other fruit.

Atoles

Atoles and other thin corn gruels have an ancient history. The dry powdered *pinole* made of toasted corn was the field ration of early Indian warriors and is still used by hunters and travelers.

Champurrado
(Chocolate-flavored *atole* drink)
Mexicans drink a lot of *atole,* a hot, thick beverage made of *masa* and spices, and often fresh fruit. These are home preparations, seldom sold in restaurants, and not especially appealing to Americans because of the corn-thickened texture. *Champurrado,* an *atole* flavored with chocolate, served very hot to accompany sweet *tamales* or the wonderful Mexican *pan dulce,* is often served steaming on cold nights. We think that part of its appeal is the fancy carved wooden *molinillo,* whirled between the hands to keep the *champurrado* from burning.

⅓ cup *masa harina*
3 cups cold water
2 tablets Mexican chocolate
(or 2 ounces dark chocolate,
1 teaspoon powdered cinnamon
and 2 drops almond extract)
2 tablespoons brown sugar
1 teaspoon vanilla
2 cups milk

1. Mix *masa harina* with one cup water. Add remainder of water, mix well, and strain through fine sieve.

2. Bring to a boil in saucepan over low heat, stirring constantly.

3. Break up chocolate tablets and add to the *masa harina* mixture with sugar and vanilla, a little at a time. Stir constantly. Add milk slowly, and cook until mixture is creamy. Serve hot. Serves about 6.

A great variety of botanicals, for teas, are prescribed by curanderas (folk doctors). Most markets are very well-stocked.

Café de Olla
(Pot coffee)

Per 2 cups water:
4 to 6 tablespoons Mexican coffee beans,
coarsely ground
1 large or 2 small sticks cinnamon
1 small *piloncillo* (or 1 tablespoon
brown sugar packed)

Place all ingredients into a saucepan and bring to a boil. Simmer 3 to 5 minutes. Bring to a second boil and again simmer 3 to 5 minutes. Strain and serve. Serves 2.

Café con Leche
(Coffee with milk)

Brew strong coffee (2 heaping tablespoons per cup). In Mexico it's often stronger, but even this may be a little strong for you.

Combine equal parts coffee and hot milk. Sweeten to taste.

Chocolate Mexicano
(Mexican chocolate)

4 cups milk or water
1 tablet Mexican chocolate, crushed

Heat liquid and add chocolate. Blend until frothy and serve. Serves 4.

Teas

Mexicans do not normally drink the black or green teas used by so much of the rest of the world. Teas of *manzanilla* (chamomile) and of *canela* (stick cinnamon), mallow, lemon grass, mint and other botanicals are made but are generally used as remedies rather than refreshments.

Infusions that might be thought of as teas are made from tamarind pods, and from jamaica flowers.

Agua de Jamaica
(*Jamaica* flower cooler)

Jamaica (pronounced hah-My-kah) or roselle is the dried, purple-red flower of a member of the hibiscus family. It can be bought in cellophane envelopes in stores in Latin areas. Mexican punch is particularly refreshing when made from *jamaica*. It is commonly served at church socials and charity events which, interestingly, are also called *jamaicas*.

½ cup (½ oz.) loose *jamaica* flowers
1 cup water
4 cups water
¼ to ½ cup sugar to taste

1. In a saucepan, place together the flowers and 1 cup water. Bring to a boil and cook over medium heat for 5 minutes.

2. Pour into a large china or glass container and add the additional water and sugar. Stir to dissolve the sugar.

3. Refrigerate 6 hours. Strain and serve over ice in tall glasses. Makes about 4 cups.

Sangría
(Wine cooler)

This summer drink from Spain is now so common in Mexico that its origins are all but forgotten. Naturally, in a land of so many tasty tropical fruits, Mexicans often add pieces of sweet banana or pineapple and a bit more sugar. In our opinion, this makes it too sweet to serve with heavy meals and better suits festive occasions.

½ lemon, in ¼ inch slices
½ orange, in ¼ inch slices
1 ripe peach, pit removed, and cut into
small pieces (substitute an apple
when peaches are out of season)
¼ cup sugar (vary to taste)
1 bottle (⅘ quart) dry red wine
1 small bottle of club soda (more,
if desired)
2 ounces brandy (optional)

Combine fruit and sugar in a large pitcher. Add wine and mix well. Chill. Before serving add the soda and brandy if desired and lots of ice. Serves 4 to 6.

Sangría is excellent for a party punch. Freeze pieces of fruit into a large ring mold of ice, or into large ice cubes, and serve in a punch bowl.

Sangría Estilo Mexicano
(Mexican style *sangría*)

½ cup sugar
1 bottle (⅘ quart) dry red or white wine
1 cup orange juice
Juice of 2 or 3 limes

Dissolve the sugar in the mixture of wine and fruit juices. Chill and serve with ice cubes, garnished with fresh fruit slices. Serves 4 to 6.

It takes 8 to 10 years for the mezcal azul *or* blue maquey (Agave tequilana) *to mature. *Tequila *is distilled from the cooked and fermented hearts of these plants.*

The pulque maguey (Agave atrovirens) *is tapped for* aguamiel (honey water) *by cutting out the central stalk before the plant blooms, usually at least 10 years after planting.*

Tequila and mezcal

The best known drinks of Mexico are made from the maquey or agave plant; *pulque* is the mildly alcoholic drink made from the sap harvested from a large maguey *(Agave atrovirens)*. It was probably used in Mexico as early as 300 A.D. If you want to try a sample you'll have to do it in Mexico. *Pulque* is consumed in its active fermenting stage, and has a very limited storage life. Chances are you won't like it anyway, at least not on the first try, not even the strawberry-flavored kind.

Mezcal is made from a number of different agaves; the best known of these is *mezcal de Tequila,* usually just called *tequila.* This is made from the *mezcal azul* (blue maguey) that grows in a limited area to the east and west of the city of Guadalajara. *Tequila* is made by distillation from the cooked and fermented hearts of the blue maguey plant. It takes 8 to 10 years for a plant to mature for harvest.

If you want to drink *tequila* in the classic way — "straight" with salt and lime — just follow this step-by-step method. Pick up a wedge of lime in the left hand and sprinkle a bit of salt in the depression formed between the base of your thumb and forefinger. If there is no depression, just lick a convenient spot on the back of the hand so the salt will stick. Now with the tequila glass in your right hand, lick the salt, down the shot and bite

the lime. (The important trick is not to breathe in until after you bite the lime!) If this seems to require too much dexterity, just have a *margarita.* Its salt-rimmed glass sort of synthesizes the same series of sensations.

(Personally, we feel that if you like *tequila* straight, you'll really love it with *sangrita* as a chaser.)

Sangrita

Sangrita is a Mexican drink that is becoming quite popular in the United States. It's often a fiery brew, not to be confused with *sangría.* There is no standard recipe. The variations are as numerous as the hosts who serve it. There are even several brands of bottled *sangrita* available on the market. Most recipes include tomatoes or tomato juice, orange juice, and hot chiles.

2 pounds tomatoes, blanched, peeled, and seeded or one 32-ounce can tomato juice
Juice of 3 oranges
Juice of 2 limes
1 small onion chopped
1 teaspoon sugar
4 to 6 fresh hot chiles, seeded, and chopped or hot chile powder, or Tabasco sauce
Salt and pepper to taste

Combine all the ingredients in a blender until smooth. Chill well before serving. *Sangrita* is generally served in tequila glasses (slightly larger than American whiskey glasses) and accompanied by glasses of tequila and slices of fresh limes. This recipe makes a little more than a quart.

Margarita Cocktail

In the southwestern United States the *margarita* cocktail has become so popular that it seriously challenges most of the more traditional mixed cocktails. There are now on the market very acceptable prepared, frozen or bottled *margarita* mixes to which only the tequila and crushed ice need be added. Though varied by many bars and restaurants by the addition of a dash of other liqueurs, the following is a good standard recipe.

2 or 3 parts white tequila
1 part Cointreau or Triple Sec
Juice of ½ lemon

Rub the rim of a chilled glass with a piece of lemon, then encrust the rim with salt by turning it in a dish of loose salt. Add the ingredients to crushed ice in a cocktail shaker, shake until frothy and strain into the prepared glasses.

The aguamiel for pulque *is still collected in the traditional manner by a* tlachiquero *and his burro.*

Index

Where to find the ingredients

Chicago

Casa del Pueblo
1810 Blue Island
Chicago, Illinois 60608

Casa Esteiro
2719 West Division
Chicago, Illinois 60622

Denver

El Molino Foods Inc.
1078 Santa Fe Drive
Denver, Colorado 80204
Tel. (303) 623-7870

Los Angeles

El Mercado
First Avenue and Lorena
Los Angeles, CA 90063

New York

Casa Moneo
210 West 14th Street
New York, New York 10014
Tel. (212) 929-1644
Mail orders
Cooking equipment

Trinacaria Importing Co.
415 Third Avenue
New York, New York 10014
Tel. (212) LE2-5567

San Antonio

Frank Pizzini
202 Produce Row
San Antonio, Texas 78207
Mail orders
Chiles, corn husks, herbs

San Francisco

La Palma
2884 24th Street
San Francisco CA 94110
Tel. (415) 648-5500

Santa Fe

Theo. Roybal Store
Rear 212-216 Galistero St.
Santa Fe, New Mexico 87501
Mail orders
Cooking equipment

Seattle

Mexican Grocery
1914 Pike Place
Seattle, Washington, 98101

La Mexicana
10022 16th, S.W.
Seattle, Washington 98146
Tel. (206) 763-1488
Some cooking ware
Tortilla factory

Washington, D.C.

Casa Peña
1636 17th Street, N.W.
Washington, D.C. 20009
Tel. (202) 632-6500

International Safeway
1330 Chain Bridge Road
McLean, Virginia 22101

Metric conversions

Approximate conversions *to* metric measures

	When you know:	Multiply by:	To find:
Mass (weight)	ounces (oz.)	28	grams (g.)
	pounds (lb.)	0.45	kilograms (kg.)
Volume	teaspoons (tsp.)	5	milliliters (ml.)
	tablespoons (Tbsp.)	15	milliliters (ml.)
	fluid ounces (fl. oz.)	30	milliliters (ml.)
	cups (c.)	0.24	liters (l.)
	pints (pt.)	0.47	liters (l.)
	quarts (qt.)	0.95	liters (l.)
	gallons (gal.)	3.8	liters (l.)
Temp. (exact)	Fahrenheit (°F) temperature	5/9 (after subtracting 32)	Celsius (°C) temperature
Length	inches (in.)	2.5	centimeters (cm.)
	feet (ft.)	30	centimeters (cm.)
	yards (yd.)	0.9	meters (m.)
	miles (mi.)	1.6	kilometers (km.)

Approximate conversions *from* metric measures

	When you know:	Multiply by:	To find:
Mass (weight)	grams (g.)	0.035	ounces (oz.)
	kilograms (kg.)	2.2	pounds (lb.)
Volume	milliliters (ml.)	0.03	fluid ounces (fl. oz.)
	liters (l.)	2.1	pints (pt.)
	liters (l.)	1.06	quarts (qt.)
	liters (l.)	0.26	gallons (gal.)
Temp. (exact)	Celsius (°C) temperature	9/5 (then add 32)	Fahrenheit (°F) temperature
Length	millimeters (mm.)	0.04	inches (in.)
	centimeters (cm.)	.04	inches (in.)
	meters (m.)	3.3	feet (ft.)
	meters (m.)	1.1	yards (yd.)
	kilometers (km.)	0.6	miles (mi.)